*India*
*The Shimmering*
*Dream*

*A captivating window to a forgotten*

MAX REISCH

CW00734410

## Also from Veloce Publishing –

An Incredible Journey – The lost world of the 1930s circled by two men in one small car (Reisch)
Bonjour – Is this Italy? (Turner)
Carrera Panamericana, La (Tipler)
*Daily Mirror* 1970 World Cup Rally 40, The (Robson)
Drive on the Wild Side, A – 20 Extreme Driving Adventures From Around the World (Weaver)
France: the essential guide for car enthusiasts – 200 things for the car enthusiast to see and do (Parish)
From Crystal Palace to Red Square – A Hapless Biker's Road to Russia (Turner)
Mini Minor to Asia Minor – There & Back (West)
Motorcycling in the '50s (Clew)
Peking to Paris (Young)
The Essential Guide to Driving in Europe – New Edition! (Parish)

# www.veloce.co.uk

This book was translated by Alison Falls from *Indien – Lockende Ferne* by Max Reisch (7th edition published in 2003) published by Ennsthaler Verlag, Steyr Ennsthaler Gesellschaft mbH.

*Indien – Lockende Ferne* was originally published in 1949 by Verlag Ullstein & Co Gesellschaft mbH. The author, Max Reisch, amended later editions (of which this is a translation) to bring it up to date.

All photographs are the copyright of the Reisch-Orient-Archiv to whom the translator and publisher are very grateful for their help in producing this English Edition.

First English edition published in 2010 by Panther Publishing. This edition first published in August 2018 by Veloce Publishing Limited, Veloce House, Parkway Farm Business Park, Middle Farm Way, Poundbury, Dorchester DT1 3AR, England. Fax 01305 250479 / e-mail info@veloce.co.uk / web www.veloce.co.uk or www.velocebooks.com.

ISBN: 978-1-787112-94-0 UPC: 6-36847-01294-6

© 2018 Alison Falls, Peter H Reisch and Veloce Publishing. All rights reserved. With the exception of quoting brief passages for the purpose of review, no part of this publication may be recorded, reproduced or transmitted by any means, including photocopying, without the written permission of Veloce Publishing Ltd. Throughout this book logos, model names and designations, etc, have been used for the purposes of identification, illustration and decoration. Such names are the property of the trademark holder as this is not an official publication. Readers with ideas for automotive books, or books on other transport or related hobby subjects, are invited to write to the editorial director of Veloce Publishing at the above address. British Library Cataloguing in Publication Data – A catalogue record for this book is available from the British Library. Typesetting, design and page make-up all by Veloce Publishing Ltd on Apple Mac. Printed in India by Parksons Graphics.

# India
# The Shimmering
# Dream

*A captivating window to a forgotten world*

MAX REISCH

# VELOCE PUBLISHING
THE PUBLISHER OF FINE AUTOMOTIVE BOOKS

# CONTENTS

Herr Schömann. Oasis without palm trees. Have we had it easy till now? Stage fright. Farewell to Duzdab.

Only another 800 kilometres to India. Dying of thirst – the greatest danger. Unpleasant calculations. Cracked cables. Rail trip by motorcycle. A deserted railway station. Nomad tents at a saint's tomb. Death breathing down our necks. The Baluchis – a strange, proud people. The first motor tracks in the sand. The wonderful wide ribbon.

Warm welcome in Quetta. Objects of interest for the harem. Installing the dynamo. Joyful farewell. A city in the desert. Invitation to Pishin. The hospitality of Sadar Joffer Khan.

Sleeping on the edge of a precipice. A hunting adventure. Sweet-sounding names. Two versus the mob. We cross the Indus. Many faces of the fairytale land. Lahore. Doctor Sondhi. Tent camp in the garden. Indian students. A precious talisman.

Amritsar, centre of the Sikhs. A strange religious group. The Golden Temple. First wash your feet. Tobacco and alcohol forbidden.

Kitchen clock at Buddha's feet. The camera falls in the water. A brilliant idea. A little flame becomes a wall of fire. Dodging the tolls. Not a good day.

Guests of the Maharajah. Secret Service in India. Excursion to the Himalaya. A python as nanny. A German forester's house in India. Chased by a tribe of monkeys. A daredevil car trip into the mountains. The back wheel goes its own way.

Two capital cities. Religion is everything. Creating a sensation in Old and New Delhi. Slow progress. Peasants, pilgrims and sacred cows. Monument to a great love. Ultimate beauty. A night in the jungle.

In Gwalior and Bhopal. With the Maharajah of Indore. Friend, advisor and philosopher. The rest of our luggage. A brother to all men. Theory and practice. The last kilometres to Bombay. We reach our destination.

# FOREWORD
# TO THE ENGLISH EDITION

Today's young men and women have potentially greater opportunity for adventure than ever before. For the young would-be backpacker, the other side of the globe is only a budget-price airfare away. Long distance motorcycle journeys undertaken by young travellers, often on slender budgets, are now quite commonplace. Riders can circle the globe without even a puncture. But what of such travel back in the early thirties? Who knows what difficulties these pioneer motorcycle travellers faced? And what is it in their stories that younger riders might benefit from today?

These were some of the thoughts which passed through my mind a few summers back when, quite by chance, I came across the story of a truly remarkable motorcycle journey undertaken by two young Austrian students, Max Reisch and Herbert Tichy. We were on a family holiday in Austria during a period of heavy rain that resulted in the disastrous flooding of much of central Europe. Among the indoor attractions we visited to keep out of the incessant downpour was an exhibition, 'Der Berg ruft' ('The call of the mountains'). Housed in a large industrial building at Altenmark near Salzburg, it was a celebration of the 'International Year of the Mountains' with many fascinating exhibits about mountain life, travel and climbing from all over the world. I have ridden motorcycles almost every day for over forty five years, and my eye was soon caught by a display which featured a most interesting early '30s Puch split single (a double piston, single cylinder 2-stroke). It had the engine mounted in line with the frame, driving the gearbox directly and a clutch in the rear wheel hub. The display board described this as an example of the machine used by Reisch and Tichy to make the first overland crossing by motorcycle from Europe to India in 1933/4.

On returning home to England I determined to find out more about the two young travellers. A search on the internet revealed that in the late '40s Max Reisch had written about this journey in a book: *Indien – Lockende Ferne*. I obtained a copy through the kind offices of an Oxford section member of the Vintage Motor Cycle Club, Dr Martin Schenker. However, I soon realised that my schoolboy German was so rudimentary that I stood no chance of understanding it. Then I managed to persuade my sister, Alison Falls, who had studied and taught the language, to translate some of it for me. Her enthusiasm for the unfolding story (and Reisch is a consummate storyteller) soon led her to translate the entire book.

Again via the internet, I made contact with Max Reisch's son, Peter, who now lives in the South Tyrol and keeps the Max Reisch Archive (see www.maxreisch.at). Reisch went on, after serving during the Second World War as a technical inspector in the Afrika Korps, to become a great international motor traveller. He was well-known for his illustrated lectures. He was also a prolific writer, producing articles for newspapers and magazines, accounts of his round-the-world journeys by car and motorcycle, and adventure stories for young people based on his own experiences.

All his life he made it his business to foster that desire to see the wide world at first hand that besets young people, especially in their late teens and early twenties. Yet his infectious enthusiasm was always tempered by rigorous planning and a sympathetic interest in the peoples and cultures he visited along the way. The glimpses he provides of life in the Middle Eastern countries along his route are illuminating and should encourage Western readers to learn more about the history of this region and cultivate that understanding between peoples which Reisch valued so highly.

**Roger Bibbings, January 2010**

# 1
# YOUTHFUL OPTIMISM

Today, when I think it all over, I am full of amazement at the directors of the Puch Works who bestowed on a callow youth one motorcycle and a tidy sum of money which they might never see again. For the goal was a distant one and success very uncertain, namely, to follow in the footsteps of Alexander the Great on Xenophon's legendary 'Road of the Army of Ten Thousand' and reach the faraway

Puch motorcycle built in 1904, owned by Max's father, Hans August Reisch, and nicknamed 'Himmelstürmer.' Now in the Reisch-Orient-Archiv, it is probably the oldest maintained long-distance machine in the world.

wonderland of India – an exciting challenge for any young man in his 'storm and stress' years.

In 1904-5 Sven Hedin had rediscovered the land route to India, riding on camelback through the deserts of mysterious Asia. Now this thirteen thousand kilometre trek was to be attempted for the first time by a modern means of transport.

In 1933 I had recently arrived in Vienna from Kufstein to study trade and transport geography. In this city of two million inhabitants I knew nobody who might help me realise my travel plan, or give me any idea how to go about it. I had neither contacts nor patrons. As for money, I had just enough to allow me the occasional excursion to the Rax mountains near Vienna, but the projected trip to India would necessitate a five figure sum. Today, I feel only the deepest gratitude to the industry, the Touring Club and the Automobile Club for taking my plans seriously. The trip cost a lot. The industry provided the money – my contribution would have been too small to show up on any company balance sheet except as a vague entry under petty cash – and my parents contributed plenty of good advice. My father even encouraged the project, more or less on the quiet. In his youth he had undertaken a similarly crazy journey – two thousand kilometres through Italy to the Ligurian Sea in 1905 on a motorcycle with no gears and no clutch! Carburation, ignition systems, the starting mechanism and slipping belt drives were the technical problems of that era. But the machine was amazingly reliable. Far greater were the troubles caused by whip-lashing coachmen, shying horses, stone-throwing *lazzaroni* (beggars) and biting dogs. But the sensation he created was colossal – for example in Bologna ... *The hotelier had the machine cleaned up and when I came into the restaurant, there stood the motorcycle next to the table that had been reserved for me. The numerous other diners were crowding round the vehicle whose red enamel and shining nickel trim made a grand spectacle.*

My father described this sensational journey in various newspapers, and it is a delight to read of the patent starting mechanism, the ignition problems, and, of course, many tyre defects. In the final instalment of this 'account of a modern motorised journey' we read ... *I had covered nearly two thousand kilometres and climbed in all over five thousand metres. It was a pleasure to contemplate the miracle of technology which had carried me like wings over hill and dale and which had justly earned the official rating 'Perfect.'*

One can see from this that everything is relative, and it is possible that my father's great Italian journey of 1905 was – from a technical viewpoint – a greater achievement than my trip to India.

Today, this Puch machine which my father called the *Himmelstürmer* ('heaven stormer') is still in the family's possession, and used to stand in the transport history section of the Tyrol State Museum in Innsbruck (now kept with the Reisch-Orient-Archiv). The curator, Dr Pizzinini, rightly considered this earliest example of an Austrian motorcycle so valuable that he had a large glass case built around it. There is also a nice postcard to be had in this museum which shows the red enamel paint and shining nickel to best advantage.

So, from my father's side came this weight of inheritance, but his attitude was quite clear. "It's all right by me, but you must raise the money yourself." Mother was very reluctant and hoped that somehow I would never succeed in realising this 'unfortunate notion.'

What I liked best as a very little boy was to lie underneath my father's car,

'In the river bed at Aulla.' The motorcycle on which Hans-August Reisch (father of Max Reisch) made a journey of over 2000 kilometres through Italy in 1905, attracting considerable attention. He wrote about the trip in a number of newspapers.

marvelling at the clever arrangement of wheels and levers. So how did I acquire this lifelong interest in motors? It was force of circumstance, certainly, and somehow it was in our blood, part of our tradition. My father's ride to the Ligurian Sea and back was probably more difficult than my entire India trip.

So you could say that a tendency to motorised journeys ran in the family. That explains where the notion came from, but turning my plans into reality was hard going. When I arrived in the big city of Vienna, in 1931 as a high school graduate, I was very wet behind the ears, but I had two ambitions. The first was to study and the second to do a 'grand journey.' The first was a perfectly acceptable, normal activity, but the second was a real challenge to my ingenuity. My old man was in favour of my project and very sympathetic, but insisted that I must raise the money for it myself. This paternal blessing given in principle was very gratifying, but did nothing to relieve my poverty-stricken situation in student digs in Vienna. Eventually I came one tiny step nearer to the realisation of my plans – I became a film courier. I don't know whether the job still exists today. It involved transporting reels of film from one cinema to another, from afternoon until late at night. My wages were 10 *Schilling* a day (very approximately £50 today). These were enormous earnings for a student part-timer, and I was soon the proud owner of a second-hand Puch 175 Sport with double exhaust pipes. On this conveyance I did a couple of holiday trips and began to write about it under the titles of *With 3hp over the Stilfersjoch* and *Easter Trip to Lake Garda*. I took the first article to Herr Köhler who was then editor of *Motorrad*

(*Motorcycle*) in the *Burggasse*. My heart beat like mad as I told him who I was and timidly handed over my sheets of paper, together with a couple of drawings I had done myself, because I had no camera then. The manuscript was handwritten, as I also lacked a typewriter.

I owe a great debt of gratitude to Herr Köhler of *Motorrad*. He actually printed my first effort and I was terribly proud of the fee offered. This first success gave me courage, and I wrote a long series of articles for another Viennese paper. Its publisher was very kind to me, which was balm for my soul, as I was seething with inferiority complexes. Each time I would be on tenterhooks until the new number came out, and blissfully happy when my next article was in it. There was a snag, of course. In spite of constant promises I never received a penny for any of these articles. At the time I simply could not understand it. As far as I was concerned, publishers, editors, even publishers' clerks, were figures of authority and I could never imagine that they would let me down in this way. Soon afterwards, the publication folded (I hope not because of my articles) and I have forgiven the publisher, the editor and the clerk long ago. But I was only eighteen years old then and considered this cheating of my travel fund to be a rank injustice. But some good came out of it. I now had in my possession a whole file of travel articles which I carried around like a priceless treasure. With unshakeable tenacity, I forced Herr Zwickl, then advertising director of Puch, to read this bumf, and, after lengthy urging, the sales director of Puch, Dr Jany, finally agreed to support my project. But which project?

My professor of trade and transport geography, for whom I had the greatest respect, and who sometimes let me chat with him in a semi-official capacity, had given an inspiring lecture on Sven Hedin's great Asian journey *Overland to India* of 1905-6. The Swede Sven Hedin had virtually rediscovered the once vital land route to India which had fallen into oblivion with the improvement in sea trade. He did this on camel-back and equipped a great caravan for the purpose. Overland to India: wasn't that just the thing for Max Reisch on a motorcycle? Professor Dietrich, who was at that time an international transport expert, shook his head thoughtfully and said, "It won't work, not yet it won't." But I'd got the bug! In Professor Dietrich's opinion, I shouldn't consider myself capable of such an attempt before building up some relevant experience. This led to my suggestion to Dr Jany of a journey to the Sahara, going through Morocco to Algeria, into the Sahara desert and back via Tripoli. He wasn't exactly wild about the idea and gave me only modest encouragement. My film-can delivery bike, which by now was a Puch 250, and already three years old, would be checked out by the Puch Works (as it was then), I would be presented with a few spare parts and a very modest cash sum. All the same, these were concrete offers and Professor Dietrich was very taken with the plan. He reckoned that a trip like this should succeed, as North Africa had been pretty well civilized by the French and Italians. I flung myself enthusiastically into preparations for this experimental ride, while never losing sight of my ultimate goal – the first motorcycle ride overland to India.

My travel companion to Africa was Alfred Schricker from Munich. I had a lot of trouble finding him, but he was ready to pay for half the petrol and also to stump up for his own rations. This was pretty generous, considering that most of the people I'd buttonholed were only prepared to take part in my strenuous project if they could travel free and be paid! Remember that motorcycle trips in those days scarcely went beyond the borders of one's own country: so once we had crossed France and found ourselves on the Spanish frontier, we felt tremendously proud and important ...

In Malaga we arrived by chance just at the beginning of a motorcycle race meeting. As guests from faraway Austria we were assigned places among the spectators right by the starting line. The 125 class went off first. Then an official suddenly came up to me and insisted on my riding in the 250 class as an honorary competitor. I thought, "Well, just for a lark ... " So I quickly took the heavier bits of luggage off the machine and lined up with the other riders. At the end of the race I nearly had piston seizure and coasted over the finishing line virtually in neutral. Believe it or not, I'd won second prize! This proves that it was only a very modest race, but still with an international line-up. It was reported next day in the newspaper that Señor Don PUCH (they didn't know my name) had won second prize. I can still produce the newspaper cutting to this day and I've got three excellent photos of the start, the race itself and the prize giving by *reporter gráphico Zarco* from Malaga. The most important thing about this race turned out to be the prize, which was a genuine silver cigarette case. Just how important it was I only found out later in Algeria when I fell off and ran the handlebars into my chest so hard that the cigarette case was seriously dented. Without this chance bit of armour-plating I would have broken a couple of ribs.

From Malaga we crossed over to Melilla in Morocco and rode through Algeria over the Tell Atlas far into the Sahara. The most beautiful oases on this tour through the desert were Bou Sada, Biskra, Touggourt and Ouargla. From Ouargla we would have ventured even further south had we not been lacking one tiny spare part. Let me explain: our tyres had bicycle valves of which the most important component was a very small rubber tube not much bigger than a matchstick. These tubes had become porous and no longer held the air in, so every day we had to keep pumping up the tyres. If these little tubes had given out altogether we'd have been stuck out in the desert with two flat pancakes. We had no replacements and French bicycle valves were constructed in a totally different way. It was a detail, but it irritated us and thwarted our youthful enthusiasm. Not until Tripolitania (a province of Libya) did we find spares that fitted.

So this trip had its fair share of adventure, more or less dicey situations and crashes, but I did learn how to handle a heavily loaded motorcycle on difficult terrain and how to get over sand dunes. I also had more than a few hard lessons in how to deal with the authorities, the local people, my travelling companion and myself.

Anyway, it was nine thousand six hundred kilometres back to Vienna via Sicily and Italy. One other thing attracted a lot of attention in the newspapers: it was the first time an Austrian motorcycle had gone beyond the frontiers of Europe! Zwickl, the publicity manager, and Dr Jany, the sales manager at the Puch Works were very pleased, and their confidence grew. There were now no technical or financial obstacles to the great India project.

In short, that is the tortuous route I had to take to get the necessary support from the industry in spite of times being 'bad' in those days. In my opinion, times are always more or less bad, when seen from the standpoint of the present. The 'good old days' are always the only good ones. In 1934 when I returned from India, a big Viennese newspaper wrote as follows:

*...When he turned up at the Urania Hall, it was sold out – which is no mean feat these days – and this proves that a daring sporting achievement today arouses just as much interest as it did a few years ago when we were beset by far fewer worries.*

So even way back in 1934, people had plenty to worry about, and were amazed that it was possible to fill a space like the Urania Hall in such 'bad times.'

A question which I am usually asked by young enthusiasts goes something like this: 'Are there still geographical challenges for motor travel that could attract the interest of the general public, not to mention financial support from industry?' I cannot see into the future, but a look at the past may go some way to providing an answer to this question.

Let us take first of all an example of geography. Sven Hedin, the like of whom we shall not see again, was twenty years old when he visited Persia and travelled the length and breadth of the country. That was in 1885, when the West had an extensive body of literature about Persia. This country was 'known.' Could anything new be brought to the subject? That is just what Sven Hedin did, so we then had 'exhaustive knowledge' of Persia. Sven Hedin's first book on Persia has been followed to date by some eighty books on the same subject by different authors, and a couple more come out each year. More or less the same can be said of every country on earth. In other words, the face of the world is constantly changing, and there will always be something new to discover and to write about.

Now, a motor travel example: Prince Scipione Borghese and his companion Luigi Barzini took part in a motorcar race from Peking right through Mongolia and Siberia to Paris. This was in 1907! How long did it take them? It sounds impossible but it really is true. They left Peking on 10th June and on 10th August they reached Paris. They took only two months in their Itala car to cover the sixteen thousand kilometres right across Asia – in 1907. This is such an exceptional achievement that no one has bettered it and, all things considered, they are unlikely to do so in the future.

Nevertheless, our motorcycle trip to India in 1933 caused quite a sensation. The illustrated journals carried full-page pictures on their covers, reports in the dailies ran into several columns, and even Max Brod, the great Viennese sports editor, who was always very sceptical, wrote a series of enthusiastic articles about our pioneering journey in the *Wiener Tagblatt* (a Viennese newspaper). The entire European press contained detailed reports of the trip and I gave more than seven hundred lectures about the journey throughout half Europe, and the halls were always packed.

I am almost embarrassed to think of Borghese's great feat in 1907, but it should be a comfort to all the unknown friends who ask my advice. My trip to India was trivial when compared with what Borghese achieved. But times change, so there will always be some new or interesting reason for making a journey.

One more question needs answering: how much did the motorcycle trip to India cost? It is not possible to express it completely in figures because of the existence of so many indirect costs. One would have to take into account the time spent in preparation, the necessity of paying tuition fees in advance, and quite a lot else. However, here is an attempt to express it in round figures.

The 1932 trip to North Africa via Spain with Alfred Schricker of Munich, undertaken as training for the big India expedition. A motorcycle race was just about to start in Malaga and we were invited to take part. The riders on the starting line, with Max Reisch in Pullman cap and goggles on his machine, number A2443 (second from left).

| | Austrian *Schilling* |
|---|---:|
| Visas, maps, literature, telegrams, etc | 1000 |
| Travelling to London to get information from the Royal Geographical Society and Automobile Association | 1500 |
| Puch 250 motorcycle | 1600 |
| Conversion of tank, handlebars, saddles and attaching cases, saddlebags and carriers | 1000 |
| Tent, mosquito nets, airbeds, other equipment | 1200 |
| Travel expenses for 4 months for 2 people Vienna-Bombay | 8000 |
| Return journey by ship Bombay – Trieste | 2000 |
| **Total** | **16,300** |

(In today's money this would represent about £80,000)

Most of this sum was contributed by industrial sponsors in Austria. On top of this, of course, came the cost of cameras, ciné equipment, films, etc.

Concerning the actual travel expenses between Vienna and Bombay (8000

*Continued on page 20*

I took part just for a lark, with all my luggage. The competition wasn't great but I was nevertheless astounded to come in second and win a cigarette case. When I crashed in the Sahara, the handlebars ran into my chest in the very spot where I had the cigarette case in my pocket. I could have broken a couple of ribs, but only dented the case. I still keep it as a mascot.

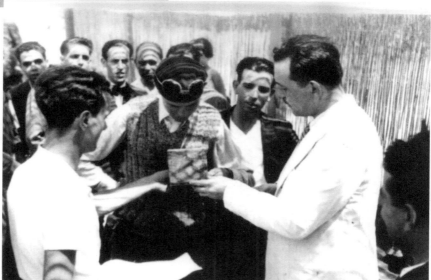

The next day in the paper it read, 'Categoria A, 250ccm, primero: Señor Calvo Robino, segundo: Señor 'Puch,' tercero: Señor Renco.' The amusing bit was that they didn't know my name, and just called me 'Herr Puch.'

This Moroccan poacher is not afraid of the motorcycle, although he has never seen one before.

In the sand dunes of the Sahara I learned how to steer a heavily loaded motorcycle. As with life, you just have to go for it! I confess that there were often lumps of stone hidden in the sand that could suddenly halt the machine's progress: then I would fly through the air and frequently end up with my face in the sand. That's how I kissed the desert and learned to love it!

One of our many camps in the Algerian plain of shotts (salt depressions). The tent was relatively large and heavy. For the India expedition I had a mini-tent made, weighing only 2 kilos. The Sahara trip provided a lot of useful insights that came in handy later on the journey to India. On the right of the picture is Alfred Schricker from Munich, my ever-cheerful companion on this tour. He was killed in the Second World War.

*Below:* At a well in the Sahara in Libya. The camel is drawing up a leather bag of water from the depths. We drank this water without a second thought and took no care at all. From this point of view the Sahara trip may have been more dangerous than the incomparably more difficult expedition to India.

*Opposite:* 'A problem: stowing the luggage.' How two people could make a long journey on one motorcycle and how they stowed the luggage was the subject of an illustrated article in the Berlin magazine 'Das Motorrad' of 2nd March 1933. It was the first time that a tank case was used, and also large hard panniers to left and right of the back wheel.

Reproduction of the cover of Austria's leading specialist magazine *Das Motorrad* (*The Motorcycle*) of November 1st 1932. The picture shows the flood plain of Wadi Kairouan in Tunisia. The Bedouin is better off than I am, holding his slippers while I guide the motorcycle on engine power through the slippery mud.

The journey home by ship from Tripoli to Syracuse in Sicily, after 9600 kilometres through Morocco, Algeria, Tunisia and Libya. It was the first time that an Austrian motorcycle had 'ventured' (as the press at home termed it) beyond the frontiers of Europe. The Puch Works too were well satisfied. I could now count on some support and began preparations for the great journey 'Overland to India.'

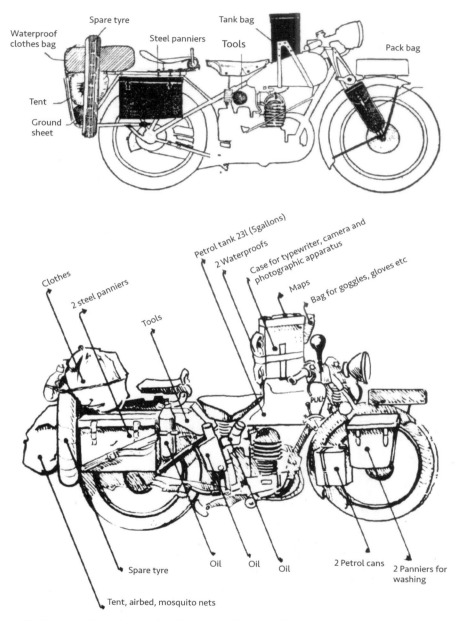

Waterproof clothes bag
Spare tyre
Steel panniers
Tank bag
Tools
Pack bag
Tent
Ground sheet

Clothes
2 steel panniers
Tools
Petrol tank 23l (5gallons)
2 Waterproofs
Case for typewriter, camera and photographic apparatus
Maps
Bag for goggles, gloves etc
Spare tyre
Oil
Oil
Oil
2 Petrol cans
2 Panniers for washing
Tent, airbed, mosquito nets

On the basis of experience gained from the Sahara trip of 1932, this improved luggage system was developed for the India expedition.

*Schilling*), I must point out that this sum could have been kept lower. The expensive bits of a trip like this are the stops in the big eastern cities – Istanbul, Baghdad, Teheran, Quetta, Lahore, Bombay – where one has to stay in especially pricey European hotels. If you keep these stops as short as possible, you will get by at significantly less expense, since living in the desert costs practically nothing at all. Out there you sleep in the tent or as the guest of some sheikh or khan.

On the other hand, we could have travelled at far greater expense. For example, if you think it is important to have food depots along the way, if you send caravans on ahead with your luggage, and hire drivers so that you can arrive at each stopping place to find an inflatable bathtub waiting for you with enough water to fill it, then it is going to cost you considerably more. On his final expedition to the Gobi desert, Sven Hedin was constantly surrounded by such comforts. There are no limits to luxury, even in the desert, provided you have the means to pay for it. On our trip we trod a middle path, not depriving ourselves of anything if the opportunity arose, but also not indulging in luxuries out of keeping with our circumstances at the time. We got on all right without the bathtub.

But back to the Indian Project. I now had finally to convince Puch to support this journey. I grew a moustache, with some effort, and spent hours at a time in my student bedsit practising the elaborate speech with which I intended to win the support of the directors of Puch. When, after having been thrown out the first few times, I actually succeeded, I was totally amazed, and simultaneously in a seventh heaven of rapture. As I came out of the door of Steyr-Daimler-Puch-AG on the *Schwarzenburgplatz*, proud as an Indian prince with my bulky India project under my arm and a considerable cash advance in my pocket, a beggar crossed my path.

In order to take weight off the back wheel, the saddle was pushed far forward. All the same, the back wheel presented big problems.

I heard him exclaim, "Must be mental!" as he made off with my banknote in his hand as fast as his old legs would carry him.

Then the machine arrived from the factory, just a normal Puch 250 straight off the production line. In those days a model like that was classed as a 'light motorcycle,' and to take it on a thirteen thousand kilometre trip though Asia was, according to all the experts, sheer madness. I wasn't too sure about it myself.

"Allah is great but this machine is not strong enough," said my Arab friend Hamy Husny Bey, a student in my year. And what about my studies? They were a burdensome additional activity and the august professors were somewhat divided in their opinions of my India project. The greybeards of course were against it. Just before my departure one of them promptly failed me in an important exam. He was quite justified in doing so, since my attendance in the lecture theatre had been very infrequent. What did I care about my classes with the prospect of India before me? And if I did by chance turn up at a lecture so that the professor could give me a 'face-wash' (student slang for making an occasional appearance in the lecture hall), my thoughts were still centred on the bright world beyond.

The company chairman had put his faith in me. That was glorious, indescribably glorious! A whole wonderful world out there was summoning me to prove myself in the university of life ...

Throughout the spring months the modest Puch 250 metamorphosed into the Indian expedition machine. The factory had simply delivered the machine in the same state as it was offered for sale to the public. Under my personal direction, various workshops in Vienna were commissioned to make the specific alterations to it that I thought necessary.

An enormous petrol tank was constructed from sheet aluminium, carrying-cases of lightweight steel and leather were attached left and right, fore and aft, above and below, and we even put a huge box on top of the petrol tank to carry the ciné apparatus and the various delicate cameras. My friend Tichy and I each had a Leica, and I also had a Rolleiflex and an old Zeiss-Ikon for 6 x 9cm roll film. The box on the tank was the best-sprung place anywhere on the machine, near to the front wheel suspension. At that time there wasn't any back wheel suspension. On the back I had them build a carrier for the tent, mosquito net, airbeds and spare tyre, and then some more petrol cans, oil bottles, and containers for water and provisions. I had to carry approximately 70 kilos of equipment, fuel and luggage, plus, on top of this pantechnicon, two human beings. Such youthful lack of consideration beggars belief! The effect was as if the little 250 cycle were carrying three people. All things considered, wasn't that a bit risky? And as for intending to travel thirteen thousand kilometres through Asia in the same fashion, wasn't that pure insanity? This machine undoubtedly came from a good stable.

Somebody asked, 'Can you actually ride this monstrosity?' A fair question, since the 'light motorcycle' weighed 193 kilos (424lb) packed and ready to go. My friend Tichy, 1.80m tall, was no featherweight, while I weighed in at 75 kilos.

At this point, I'd better introduce my fellow traveller. It wasn't too easy to find a person who was – let's be honest – crazy enough to take part in such an enterprise. A happy chance threw me together with Herbert Tichy, a young geology student. He had the same obsession as I did – to get to India at all costs. He couldn't ride a motorbike and didn't even own one, nor had he been able to get anyone else interested in his plans, but he was looking for a partner and had made up his mind that as a last resort he would cycle to India alone. I must have appeared to him as something of a *deus ex machina*, and my pillion, compared with a hard pushbike saddle, must have seemed as inviting as a feather bed. Later in Baluchistan, when the saddle springs were broken, he was heard to make a few hostile remarks concerning motorbikes, but India's asphalt roads soon mollified him.

We had no inkling then of all the difficulties to come, in spite of the direst prognoses from all the experts. A friend of my father's who had travelled widely in the Orient, when asked what he thought of our undertaking, replied thus, "Well, I suppose it's one way of committing suicide, but a very expensive and time-consuming one. Your son could do it much more simply at home."

We certainly outraged many experts and incurred a deal of criticism. Here is a letter written by Herr Ehlers, the Austrian Consul in Teheran, to Herbert's father:

I have received your communication of the 23/9 and hereby inform you that your son reached Teheran safely. He has since left again, heading for Meshed. It was possible to pass on all your correspondence. As far as I was able, I prevailed upon the travellers to refrain from doing anything stupid out of mere sensation-seeking, although I very likely incurred the wrath of both young men in the process. It is a fact that dangers abound the farther east one goes, and these are to be avoided, since it is in nobody's interest to run risks deliberately; in particular, young people such as your son and Herr Reisch must be carefully protected. I hope that my actions will have coincided fully with their parents' intentions, even if the two young men were not exactly satisfied.
Your humble servant,
Ehlers, Teheran, 15/10/33

There was certainly no lack of people warning and doubting. They expressed themselves according to temperament. When we made a trial run, fully loaded, through the streets of Vienna, the strangely equipped vehicle attracted considerable attention. At a road junction which had just been closed by the traffic policeman, a coachman pointed at me and shouted out, "Officer, look, look, that didn't oughter be allowed!"

But in many respects I was more careful than my carping critics might have supposed. We had ourselves immunised against typhus, cholera, plague and smallpox. The plague and cholera inoculations in particular took a long time and were very painful. Furthermore, I had letters of introduction to Arab sheikhs, Persian khans and Indian princes in my pocket, and in spite of appearing outwardly unconcerned, I did a whole lot of things to ensure the success of the trip. All the same, many 'unknown factors' remained, which are in any case inseparable from the very notion of an expedition. I thought, well, if luck deserts me, I just won't come back. I only have the one machine, and everything hangs on its functioning properly. I only have ten litres of water with me and the deserts of Asia are without pity.

Today, when I look back on it all, it does seem a bit foolhardy, even to me. I'll be recounting later on what a very close run thing it sometimes was. For example, in the inferno of sand and sun in Baluchistan, we would cheerfully have given away all our possessions, and I mean everything – the expensive film camera, the typewriter, both the Leicas, the Rolleiflex, even the most precious thing we had at the time, namely the films that had already been exposed – just for a dozen spokes: a dozen spokes costing a couple of *Schilling* (approximately £10 in today's money), but which for us spelt the difference between life and death.

Then later when I was going round the world in relative comfort in the Steyr 100 car, I found myself saying, "Wow, going on that motorcycle to India, I wouldn't try that again, not for all the money in the world."

27th July, 1933. We were all a bit on edge. Quite a crowd of people had turned up to see us off. I wasn't too happy about that, as it's nerve-racking to be awarded a medal before winning the race. A string of vehicles accompanied us on our progress to Kittsee on the Hungarian border. Here our troubles began: problems with the customs over the ciné camera and the spare tyre. Telephone calls to Vienna and to Budapest. A fine way to start!

But a few hours one way or the other doesn't matter too much on a journey lasting half a year, so we took ourselves off to the nearest bar and celebrated our departure. The wine flowed freely and some tears were shed. Even I had a lump in the throat. You can work up a splendid melancholy when it comes to taking leave of all the pleasures and conveniences of European civilisation, not to mention taking leave of another person (but that has nothing to do with this story).

The last moments before setting out on a great journey afford telling glimpses into the psyche of those saying their farewells. Take for instance the deeply concerned – usually relatives – "Take quinine every day when you get to the malaria zones – go slowly – if one of you gets bitten by a snake, the other must suck out the wound." The more adventurous made heavier demands, "Ride through the Syrian desert in a single day – that'll be a marvellous record." Most revealing were those who appeared to be hungry for knowledge, "You must find out whether Gandhi really lives just on goat's milk – get an invitation from a maharajah – when you come back, mind you know all about *nautch* girls," and many other curious requests which were only whispered into our ears. If we had followed up all these commissions, we would probably never have got to India, or we would very likely still be busily employed out there. Nevertheless we didn't disappoint their thirst for knowledge when we returned. You learn so many things on a journey like that, and if you don't happen to have picked up any of the specialist knowledge your questioner requires, then, knowing what he wants to hear, you can always dress up your tale with a few exotic touches.

Our waiting time slipped by rather fast. After a couple of hours we staggered out of the cosy bar, and the detached observer might have remarked that we had all put away one too many. So at last we made our start for the miraculous East. To this day I can't explain how it happened, but after only a few metres we ended up lying together with the bike in the ditch next to the customs house. The disgrace of it! I was horribly ashamed and the customs men were grinning all over their faces. Somebody muttered something about 'young fools' and a third party volunteered the following calculation, "It's sixty kilometres from Vienna to Kittsee. 13,000 divided by 60 makes 217 crashes. So you see," he opined cheerfully, "if this goes on all the way to India, there's not going to be much left of you ..."

We gathered up our pantechnicon. It was so heavy that I couldn't get it upright on my own. Helpers and onlookers stood around with serious and sad expressions. I noticed at once that the forks were bent but I said nothing about it and we both reseated ourselves on the monster.

Amid hesitant calls of "goodbye" and "be seeing you," I got the machine moving and succeeded in getting out of sight of our friends without falling off again. Thank God, the India Expedition was under way ...

Max Reisch (right) and Herbert Tichy leaving Vienna on 27th July 1933.

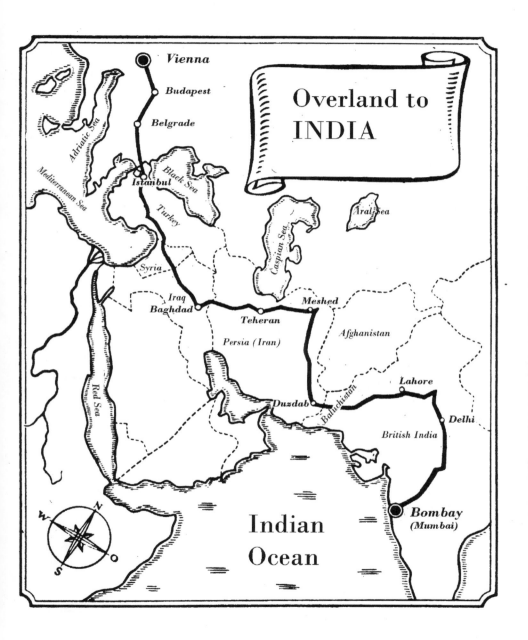

# 2
# WHERE DOES ASIA BEGIN?

Malicious gossip has it that Asia begins just beyond Vienna. There may be some truth in this. The plain we were riding over already had an Asiatic look to it, wide open and endless. The people, too, were fond of sitting on their doorsteps, and pursued their daily tasks in a calm and leisurely way. They seemed to differ little from the Austrians who show no excessive haste either. Hungarians do, after all, have a dash of central Asian blood in their veins.

Their domestic animals had certainly acquired the calm Asiatic mood: the geese, pigs and cows moving along the road regarded us as intruders into their personal kingdom. They made way for us without enthusiasm, unlike the timid animals of Austrian country roads. However, compared with the camels of Persia and the buffalo of India they were models of good behaviour and every traffic policeman's dream. Here was something else we learned on our travels – all concepts are relative.

In Budapest we had the forks straightened and spent our time in glum reflection. Our morale was at zero. India seemed to have retreated to an impossible distance. On top of this came a letter from Steyr-Daimler-Puch AG in Vienna full of instructions.

The bike still wouldn't run straight and was scarcely ridable. That meant the frame was bent too! The tank had to come off so that the alignment could be made. When it was all done, I took the monster in charge again. Soon things were looking up, and we pressed on through the Balkans, unsure as to whether we were in Europe or Asia.

First we rode over the *puszta*, which stretches away without end in all directions. You can look in vain for a landmark, as far as the eye can see in those featureless surroundings. Sometimes a cloud of dust arises, far off on the horizon, maybe approaching, maybe chasing behind you, one of the rare motor vehicles in this land of oxen and horses. We had said goodbye to metalled roads in Budapest.

The customs check at the Yugoslav border was no easy matter, and took up two hours which seemed to us an awfully long time, but then our experience of guards at the Turkish and Persian borders was yet to come.

The roads in Yugoslavia are not bad, but they have one remarkable peculiarity. Horse-drawn traffic in level country does not use the made-up road, but instead goes on the so-called 'by-roads.' These are often twenty to forty metres wide and run parallel to the main roads. They consist of rows of deep, well-worn wheel ruts

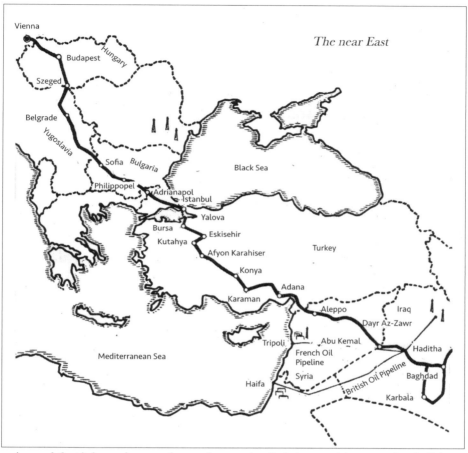

*The near East*

in sand that is knee-deep, and even the weariest little horse whips up a cloud of dust that would do credit to any sleek racing car.

At Peterwardein we rode for a while beside the Danube which is here nearly twice as wide as in Vienna, with only a sluggish current. The way at this point – with the best will in the world it couldn't be called a road – became very odd. It broke up into a number of field tracks which either met up again further on or ended in sand: it was a question of luck as to whether we got through or had to keep turning back. At last we reached Semlin. People on the road stared after us open-mouthed. Apparently a motorbike was not an everyday sight here. We crossed over the ferry to Belgrade, the grey water of the Danube and the green water of the Sava flowing side by side, sharply distinguished, and so we reached the second capital city of our trip.

A few modern streets with tall buildings, a relaxed southern feel, and very bad cobble stones – those were our superficial impressions. And then we were off again. Two days in mountainous country through Serbia and Macedonia provoked brief nostalgia for the distant mountains of our homeland, and then we were in Bulgaria.

Sofia gave us a foretaste of oriental hospitality. The Vienna newspapers, full of detailed and sceptical reports of our departure, were still widely read here, and as a result we were constantly being accosted in the street by total strangers saying, "So you want to ride to India. That's still a long way from here, but you mustn't miss having a good look round Sofia: there's the Rila monastery, my rose garden, etc ..."

However, after a couple of enforced days' rest we got going again. No doubt we incurred several debts of politeness as a result of these touching acts of hospitality, but in the first place, we did not have unlimited time at our disposal, and in the second, it was very hard to get excited about Sofia when we were dreaming about the courts of Indian maharajahs. Maybe it was not just the longing for India but also, although I wouldn't swear to this, a feeling of obligation. I had given myself the task of getting the Puch all the way to India, and Sofia was only a very early stage of that journey. How could I let myself be cosseted here, only a short hop from Vienna, when the board of directors were looking forward to our first report from Asia?

Blood in the Balkans, especially political blood, runs hotter than ours. A German friend told us the following story. He had made friends with a Macedonian and went with him to a coffee house for some talk and a few cups of coffee. After they had been sitting there for a while, the Macedonian asked to change places with him. Having done so, the Macedonian pulled out a revolver as calmly as you please and shot dead another customer, also a Macedonian. Then he allowed himself to be arrested quite peacefully, apologising meanwhile to the German for the disturbance – he called it a 'political' disturbance. When asked what he thought was the most beautiful thing in Sofia, the German replied without hesitation, "The eight o'clock express to Vienna." This reminded us that we were still, so to speak, in the shadow of St Stephen's and we made haste to be on our way again, in the opposite direction, of course.

It was raining and the poor road was transformed into a morass. On the way to Philippopel (Plovdiv) darkness overtook us in a forest. It was a rainy night and there was a thunderstorm. We would have been glad of a roof over our heads, but although we struggled on along the flooded road, not a house was to be found. At last we spotted a light up ahead.

"I can't wait for that warm stove," said Herbert, "I shall strip down to the buff and hang up my clothes until they're really dry."

"I'm going to drink a litre of hot milk," I said, "and probably a few glasses of *Schnaps*. All the peasants here keep *Schnaps*."

"*Schnaps* for me too," said Herbert, "and I fancy scrambled eggs. All the peasants here have eggs."

"I'll eat scrambled eggs too," I said, and we continued to fantasise about this lavish banquet.

Then we came to the kindly light. It was more than a light, it was a blazing fire, but it was not emanating from cheerily illuminated windows but from a single tree all in flames. It must have been struck by lightning a short time before and was blazing like a giant torch against the rainfilled sky. It made such an impressive and beautiful sight that we spared few regrets for the idea of the farmhouse, now definitely abandoned in the grey rain, and we pitched our tent near the tree, although at a safe distance.

The next day it was still raining and the engine absolutely refused to start. I checked the carburettor and blew through the jets. No problem with the petrol. It had to be the ignition. I took out the plug and checked the spark. There was a spark all right, but it looked a bit feeble to me. Anyhow, after a long time pushing, we got the engine running but it was still raining and every time we stopped for a bit it was the same carry-on. Herbert was annoyed and I was racking my brains as to why the magneto was producing such a weak spark. It was quite by chance that I discovered what the matter was: the ignition cable was jammed under the tank and squashed completely flat! This must have happened when the frame was realigned in Budapest and now, in wet conditions, the current was leaking. I got the tank off, released the cable and insulated it carefully. With everything back in working order, I was delighted. Even Herbert began to enjoy the journey once more, although whenever things like this happened later on, I couldn't avoid the suspicion that he sometimes gave a thought to the cycle trip to India he had planned for himself.

The peasants were very hospitable, but in these parts Bulgarians and Macedonians live side by side, and they are by no means so gracious to one another. We were told the following story. Once upon a time, the Lord God was taking a walk in Bulgaria and stopped at a farm. The farmer showed the distinguished visitor all over his estate and apparently made such a good impression on his guest that the latter promised to grant him one wish, on condition, however, that his next door neighbour should receive the same in double measure. The peasant sat for some minutes with furrowed brow, deep in thought. At last his face brightened and, running to the kitchen, he fetched a great knife. "Lord," he begged, "put out one of my eyes!"

In view of our increasingly annoying experiences at border crossings, we grew somewhat nervous as we approached Turkey. Up until now we had only experienced difficulties upon entering a new country, but this time a surprising novelty cropped up in the frontier procedure. It seemed that there was 'something' wrong with the visa we had got from the Bulgarian Consulate in Vienna. We never found out exactly what it was, but there must have been 'something' amiss with it or the Bulgarian official would not have kept telephoning to Sofia and insisting that we were not allowed to leave the country. Whether in the end it was the high command in Sofia or whether it was our deliberately obsequious politeness to the officials that persuaded them to let us go on, we never knew. We shot away like a bat out of hell as soon as the customs man raised the barrier, but we didn't get far. After a hundred metres or so, our way through no man's land was interrupted by another barrier. Now we really were at the gates of Turkey.

It was an idyllic scene: a tiny little hut for the border guard, lost in the flat expanse of what was now the real Asian steppe, the barrier across a road that wasn't a road but just two faint narrow wheel tracks, and the timeless, soporific expanse of the steppe stretching away in all directions. We approached the second barrier with a sense of foreboding.

We were received by a dignified man who began to examine us in a bored sort of way. He kept one hand on the barrier so that by applying just a little pressure, he could have opened it. This he did not do, however. He kept it closed and glanced at his wristwatch with the air of an outraged prima ballerina.

"Nearly seven o'clock," he said.

"Six," I said.

"Late in the evening, anyway," said the customs guard.

"It stays light for another two hours," I said.

"Nobody works in the twilight," he said.

"Would you please open the barrier," said Herbert, "so that we can get off the bike?"

"I will indeed," said the Turk, and we smiled thankfully at him. This display of cheerfulness seemed to put him in a bad mood again and he said threateningly, "but only as a personal favour so that you will not have to return to Bulgaria," jerking his head westward with a derisive movement, "I'm not doing any more work today. A person can't work all hours."

"You are quite right," I said, "we will gladly wait until tomorrow."

It was a fine dry evening. The Turk had brought out a chair from the hut and squatted on it cross-legged. He had a serene and peaceful air and paid us no more attention. We lay down in the long grass and looked skywards. Slowly, it grew dark. At last the guardian of the Turkish frontier broke his silence.

"Tomorrow is Sunday," said he, with malicious enjoyment.

"Yes?" we queried, expecting the worst.

"I don't work on Sundays," he said, giving us a triumphant look.

I remembered the name of the Turkish trade secretary – long forgotten now, but I was well acquainted with it then because he was often mentioned in the press. I spoke this name in a low voice a few times, with the best Turkish accent I could muster.

"What's that about the Secretary?" asked the Turk.

"He'll be wondering why we are so late arriving."

"Why should he wonder?"

"We're friends. He invited us to stay with him."

"Oh," he said.

Much was contained in this 'oh,' expressing simultaneously amazement, awe, annoyance, devotion to duty and a small grain of doubt. He was silent again for a while. "It's too late today," he decided at last, "You can't go any further. It's a good road, but not so very good." We regarded the sand-covered wheel tracks in the steppe and nodded. "But you can go on tomorrow morning. I will do the official business now. May I see if you have anything to declare?"

Maybe he wanted to be revenged on us for disturbing his evening siesta; maybe he hoped that we would give an account of his zeal to the Trade Secretary; maybe we were the first travellers he had been able to search for weeks and weeks, and the 'official business' marked a high point in his life; whatever the reason, I have never endured longer border formalities, and since then I've been across a lot of borders.

When we had packed our things in Vienna, we were convinced that we were only taking what was absolutely necessary. Only now, as we fetched one object after another out of the carrying-cases, passed it to the official for inspection and gave our explanations, did we realise how excellently equipped we were – generously, too. A considerable area of steppe was soon covered with our belongings, since the Turk would not allow us to stack up the things he had already seen. They had to be laid out neatly side by side so that he could cast an eye over the whole lot from time to time. The moon stood high in the night sky by the time we were allowed to pack up again. At sunrise we rode on our way.

We are still in Europe, but the Balkans with their horrendous roads and proverbial disorder have caused us some anxiety. The Bulgarian customs officers refused to let us leave the country. What had we done wrong?

"*Bon voyage, bon voyage,*" called the Turk over and over, bowing and smiling. This was our first encounter with the famous 'Asian smile', and we perceived immediately that in the face of it one is completely powerless. The best thing is to practise the new art oneself, so we smiled back, not too broadly, but pleasantly enough, calling out, "*Merci, merci, merci,*" and that's how we got into Turkey.

We were now only a few hundred kilometres from Istanbul which we longed so much to see, but then came an obstacle we had not reckoned with: the Turkish military zone.

According to regulations, the Turkish military zone could only be crossed if we carried an armed soldier. We explained that, with our machine, this was impossible. We were promptly deposited, together with the bike, in the courtyard of an army barracks and abandoned like a suitcase in the left luggage office. After a few hours we gave in and realised that this was no way to get to India. We resigned ourselves to the impossible: a soldier took his place on the pillion and Herbert climbed up behind on the tent, and off we set, three up, bumping over the rough Turkish tracks. The strange load frequently threatened to tip over. My brow was bathed in sweat from sheer fear. At any moment I felt that the whole machine would break in half. I could not bring myself to consider such an ignominious end. "Did you hear what happened to those chaps who thought they could ride to India? Didn't even make it to Istanbul ..."

I couldn't let it happen. I gritted my teeth and drove the double load in first gear at full throttle along the dusty track. This went all right as long as the steppe remained level, but then it became undulating, and on the first rise, we stuck.

The soldier was the good old-fashioned sort. His orders were to keep his eyes on us all through the military zone, and he intended to stick to those orders, however many days it took. Eventually we hit on a solution that suited him too. First, I would ride ahead carrying the soldier while Herbert followed behind on foot. Sometimes I'd go just a few hundred metres, sometimes over a kilometre, just as long as we could still keep Herbert in view. As soon as he was no more than a speck in the distance, the soldier would thump me energetically on the shoulders and point back suspiciously at Herbert. I noted with amusement that the fortifications hereabouts must have been massive but so cunningly concealed that we never saw a thing except grass and a couple of storks! But leaving Herbert too long to his own devices always ended up making our Turkish escort decidedly jumpy, so I would rush off and bring back Herbert under the watchful eye of authority. Then the whole game would be played all over again. It was terribly funny, but at the same time nerve-racking. The soldier had a rifle and looked very suspicious. Suppose I had had a breakdown as I was riding back without him, would he have believed that this was the innocent reason for stopping and waited until we got back to him, or would he have presumed the worst and fired on us just to be sure? What did we know about a Turkish soldier's sense of duty? The physical strain of such a journey was nothing to the psychological torment, but somehow our luck held, and we got ourselves, the bike and our third passenger safely to Istanbul – thanks be to Allah!

Istanbul is a glorious city. I could go on about it for hours, the way the slim towers of the minarets pushed up over the horizon like sharp needles as we came ever nearer, or the even more lovely view of the city in silhouette seen from the straits of the Golden Horn, or Hagia Sophia, that marvellous building, half church, half mosque, symbolising the not always peaceful meeting of two worlds and two religions. Or I could tell of the daily life of Istanbul, as much as a traveller on a fleeting visit can see of it. Talking together on the streets, we had to shout at one another, but nobody noticed, since it was drowned out by the bellowing of countless vendors of fruit, shoe laces, water and more, all crying their wares at the top of their voices. Through it all came the continuous noise of motor horns, which was loudest where the street was empty and straight – probably a joyful reaction. Down by the Bosphorus I saw a car driver on a completely empty street with a clear view, driving slowly along, singing a song in a deep bass voice and giving alternate blasts on horn or hooter as the melody seemed to demand – not a beautiful sound but certainly loud.

In stark contrast to this was the calm and aristocratic composure of the old Turks. Crowds of them sat pleasurably outside the coffee houses in the sun. The Stamboul coffee house is not to be compared with the sort of well-ordered little establishment that you might find in the Viennese suburbs. In Istanbul you get a few rickety chairs and sometimes a table of the same sort set down between the wall of a house and the street traffic. Here, for a few pence you can get the world-famous Turkish coffee. A drink for the gods! A small cup full of a thick aromatic fluid, it is drunk in tiny sips. If at the same time you allow your footwear to be worked on by one of the countless shoeshine boys who, carrying the tools of their trade on their back are forever on the lookout for dusty shoes, then you will already have learned the rudiments of oriental *dolce far niente*.

No, on second thoughts that is just Western arrogance. One look at the Turkish café clientele is enough to remind you that you'll always be a rank amateur in the art. There is no way to come anywhere near their professionalism. There they sit in silence, their gaze seeming to pierce the seething traffic and the walls of the buildings and to fix on some distant goal that we can never reach. Now and then they draw on the long hookah, nearly a metre tall, and take another sip from the tiny cup. And while their faces bear an expression of infinite peace, their hands are engaged in busy activity, playing with a row of amber beads, a chaplet with the ninety-nine names of Allah – the essential requisite for every respectable citizen of Istanbul. A chaplet is a long string of beautiful big amber beads which slip smoothly and adroitly through the fingers, one after the other in an endless round. The busy hands and the calm faces seem to belong to different people, but maybe the mechanical activity of the hands is a precondition for the serenity of the face. Perhaps we should have provided ourselves with amber beads before ordering our Turkish coffee.

Beads are used here not just to get rid of unwanted thoughts but also evil spirits. These are not as fine as the strings of amber, just wretched little strings of blue glass beads, often in no more than fives or threes, so that they scarcely deserve being called a string, but they are said to ward off bad luck. Tied to a halter, they keep the horse from falling or breaking a leg; attached to sheep or goat bells they keep the animals healthy and make their fleeces thick and their milk rich; on a car radiator they protect against breakdowns. They are a panacea for the trials and tribulations of fate.

We had read a lot about Istanbul in travel books, but as frequently happens with such accounts, we now found only a little of what was described. We looked apprehensively for the hordes of wild dogs that according to most books roamed the streets and from which no one in the city was safe. We had feared the worst for our pneumatic tyres and for our legs. Now, not one of these half-savage creatures was to be seen, only the occasional delicate Pekinese, out walking on a lead held by its elegant mistress. Had the books misled us again? We made enquiries of friends. No, this time they were quite right. Only a few years before, Istanbul and the surrounding area was well known for its huge packs of half wild, half starving dogs. Although everyone wanted to get rid of this plague, it was difficult to reconcile the commandments of Mohammed with those of hygiene and safety. The killing of dogs was a controversial matter. Then a resourceful individual came up with the following solution: all the dogs were rounded up and transported to a barren island in the Sea of Marmara, where they partly starved to death and partly ate each other up. Thus Istanbul was freed of its plague of dogs, without transgressing the commandments of The Koran. However, long after that, so it is said, sensitive people could remember the terrible howling that came over the water from that previously idyllic little island, especially at night.

It was incomprehensible to us how Turkish ears could be offended by even the most atrocious sounds. That extraordinary cross between groaning and shrieking which never failed to get under our skins and made us look round in alarm to see who was drowning, was only the latest number one in the Bosphorus hit parade.

Istanbul is certainly a city full of curiosities. It is also the city with the worst road surfaces. If you haven't seen this, you can't begin to imagine it. You begin by cursing Istanbul's streets, then comes enlightenment, born out of sheer necessity: you ride on the tramlines. Some people are of the opinion that this is dangerous with a bike, but once the initial nervousness has been overcome, it works like a dream, providing that the weather is dry and that you avoid the points. I was very pleased when I learned how to ride the tramlines. It proved to me that I was at last in control of our monstrosity of a bike. Riding tramlines is a sport with a charm all its own – you glide along the smooth ribbon of steel as if hovering on air, gazing contemptuously sideways at yawning pits and holes a foot deep.

*VISIT VELOCE ON THE WEB – WWW.VELOCE.CO.UK*
*All current books • New book news • Special offers • Gift vouchers • Forum*

34

# 3
# ANNOYANCES IN ANATOLIA

The next part of our journey through Asiatic Turkey, diagonally across Anatolia, was one long struggle with Turkish officialdom. Some government committee in its wisdom had decided that all travel documents should be closely scrutinised in every single village. This became ever more tedious, and, with an average of six to eight inspections a day, it wasted a huge amount of time. In Istanbul we had acquired a Turkish letter of recommendation, identifying us as friends of Turkey and of Kemal Pasha, the then head of state, and this now came in useful. Whenever we got dragged off to a police station and the check was about to begin, it was generally possible to find some fault with one of the soldiers. Either a couple of buttons would be missing from his uniform, or it would be torn. In this case, the battle was almost sure to be won. We would thrust the letter of recommendation under the man's nose and say that if we were not allowed to proceed immediately, we would write to our friend the *Ghazi* (Kemal Pasha Atatürk) and tell him about the slovenliness we had encountered.

On one occasion a man came riding after us – a horse was much faster than a motorbike on Anatolian roads in those days – and demanded that we turn back to Konya in order to have an inoculation. We were not at all keen on this idea, in the first place because we had already been immunised, in the second because it would make our arms swell up so much that we would be unable to ride for several days and in the third because I was distinctly suspicious of Asian hypodermic syringes. The soldier stuck close alongside us. What do you do in such a situation? There's a simple solution: a hard jab on the kickstarter accompanied by a sudden quick twist of the accelerator. The engine roars and the startled horse rears up and gallops away taking the rider with him, never to be seen again!

Actually, we were still in Istanbul, and I want to tell this story in the right order. In order to get to Syria, which was the next stage of our journey, two ways were open to us. The northern one led through Izmir and Ankara. We would have liked to see Ankara, the modern capital founded by Atatürk on the Anatolian steppe for strategic reasons and probably also for reasons of cultural politics. Shortly before his death he is reputed to have said that he had had few regrets in his life, but he felt that it had been a mistake to site Turkey's capital where it was subject to the icy winters and scorching summers of the Anatolian steppe.

We would certainly have liked a glimpse of modern Ankara, but at Izmir there was another military zone. The soldier who had come with us through the prohibited area before Istanbul had been thin, but suppose his Asian colleague was heavy? In view of this unpleasant possibility, we chose the southerly route.

Our steamer sailed from Yeni-Kopru, the 'new bridge' on the Golden Horn, bound for Yalova, a little seaside resort on the coast of Asiatic Turkey. This steamer trip of three hours was the only time we travelled by sea in our entire expedition. The rest of the way was covered entirely on land. We slid past the wonderful Princes' Islands where the wealthy of Istanbul have their luxury villas, and even the poor manage to find the ideal bathing beach at weekends, and the sun-scorched hills ahead of us grew bigger and took on many and varied forms. Houses became visible and this was Yalova, jumping off point for our intrepid ride through Asia.

We pushed the machine ashore and were immediately surrounded by a crowd of people. We were not the object of curiosity, but the motorcycle. The impression it made on the locals had undergone several transformations: in Vienna it was a motorcycle with a funny tank and a lot of saddle-bags, but it was still just a motorcycle which only amazed the experts, while simply causing ordinary people to pass rude remarks about it. In the Balkans it had been an odd sort of carriage, slower than a car but on the whole faster than a donkey, and worth a bit more attention than either. Here in Asia it was a miracle incarnate. Of course, people had seen motor-

Fed up with the constant police checks in villages in Anatolia, we made a detour around one village where the policeman caught us on horseback, which he did easily over the bumpy roads.

cars before, but never with two wheels. Westerners certainly had some funny ideas. "Come on, come and see the two-wheeled car before it drives away, come quickly before it goes! Don't worry, it can't go yet, we'll keep it here till you've all seen it!"

The Yalova police showed such consternation at the crowd that they forgot to check our passports, an occurrence never to be repeated. They scattered the inquisitive by laying into them with truncheons and so we got on our way.

We rode eastwards along the northern flank of Olympus, its 2500m high peak hidden in cloud. The road was enlivened by the presence of donkey caravans and buffalo carts. Although Turkish women in Istanbul strode through life in a self-confident, western manner on their high heeled shoes, here they went barefoot and veiled without exception. Only a tiny slit revealed the eyes, and even this was hastily pulled together as we came in sight. A small incident provided us with another example of Turkish phlegm. I had been riding a bit too fast and the sudden appearance of a deep irrigation ditch proved our undoing. Over the verge we went, whizzing through the air in a high arc into a field of onions where an old peasant happened to be working. No damage resulted from the crash but it must have seemed spectacular to an onlooker. I ended up at the old man's feet and was able to observe him closely. The engine which had stuck on full throttle in the crash was making a hellish din. The peasant gave us a single bored glance but carried right on working and paid no more attention to us. Time and again we encountered this

Arriving in Yalova, a town in Asian Turkey. A 'two-wheeled car' has never been seen here before. The policeman is fending off inquisitive onlookers.

Nearly all the bridges in Asian Turkey (Anatolia) were rotted through and half derelict. In summer it was safer to ride through the shallow rivers.

complete lack of interest, the very opposite of insatiable childlike curiosity, and it was quite hard to understand.

Apart from this, the roads remained good, the only difficulty being that the brooks flowed straight across them. The water was usually cloudy and we could not see through it, and this could lead to unpleasant surprises if we tried to go through at high speed. At lower speeds we got stuck, so whatever we did was wrong.

We camped for the first time in Asia on an idyllic site between two brooks. The next morning we rode through an area strongly reminiscent of our own alpine foothills, low pleasant hills with fertile fields in the valleys. Only the inhabitants transformed it into an oriental picture. The road went constantly uphill, and soon we found ourselves at a height of about 1000m. The mountains were left behind and the steppe extended all around us. Sometimes we went for an hour or two without seeing a human settlement, then the road would run for long stretches between cornfields. The threshing floors were always in close proximity to a village. For hundreds of metres there was corn, laid out in small circular areas. On each of these circles a pair of oxen drew a wooden sled with pebbles set into its underside. They went round for hours at a time, and in this way separated the grain from the ears. Only the women and children looked after these sleds (the men attended to the heavy work in the fields), sitting silent and still like black ghosts on their strange wagons, never stopping on the journey to nowhere.

The people everywhere showed a touching hospitality: the children brought us melons from the fields and the peasants, at whose table we ate bread and eggs, would not hear of any payment, and it needed our most persistent powers of persuasion to talk them into taking a few coins.

In the town of Afyon Karahisar, which lies at the foot of fantastically shaped mountains, we had to go through yet another exceptionally lengthy inspection. Scarcely had we left the town in the late afternoon than the police stopped us again. This check was soon done with, but as it was already getting dark, we put up our tent in the courtyard of an old ruined building which also housed the police station. We were invited by gestures to share the gendarmes' supper. We showed our eagerness with such energy that a short time later we were sitting at a low table. Ho, we thought, now at last for something other than bread and eggs. Then the door opened and our hosts brought in enormous thin flatbreads and sat down with us. Feeling rather depressed, we began to chew the tasteless bread. Was it true that Atatürk's reforms had been carried so zealously into effect that officials lived more modestly than the peasants? We were already fearing the worst when the door opened a second time and, as the friendly gendarmes revelled in our surprise, two men brought in a dish as big as a cartwheel containing a whole sheep roasted with rice and pumpkin seeds. There were no knives or forks, and each of our eight hosts immediately began to tear off the piece of meat that he found most desirable. Somewhat taken aback at first, we soon grasped the seriousness of the situation, and each of us quickly seized a shank and held tightly on to it. At last we emerged triumphant and were able to tuck into our spoils. However, by the friendly smiles of our hosts we soon realised that they had not been taking the contest seriously at all, and that their simulated tug-of-war with the mutton shanks had only been occasioned by the nature of the banquet so that we would not be held back by politeness.

Then began such a lip-smacking, snapping and spitting as quite exceeded our wildest expectations. After about half an hour, all that was left of the good fat sheep was its skeleton.

The next day, our road was significantly worse, with a covering of dust that came up to our footrests. Often we had to go for whole kilometres in first gear. A broad silver patch shimmered ahead of us on the horizon, a dried-up lake which had left a layer of salt looking from a distance exactly like a flawless expanse of snow. Even on this, our third day in Asia, we were unable to reach Konya, and made camp twenty kilometres from the town. As a setting for a tale from *The Arabian Nights*, our camp site could not have been bettered: a little spring with a pool beside it, a few tall poplar trees and in the distance, the bare purple mountains which ringed the plain.

At night in the tent it was bitterly cold. Here on the plateau in high summer we suffered more from cold than from heat. We were glad to be warmed by the sunbeams while they were still low as we reached Konya next morning, our first staging post in Asia Minor, six hundred and fifty kilometres from Istanbul. Konya was the dreariest town we had seen up till now. Situated in a plain almost barren of vegetation, it is at the mercy of both hot sun and wintry storms. Apart from the inevitable passport check, we also lost a great deal of time filling up with fuel. This was always a very difficult business, since petrol here was not sold in litres but by the *occa* (about one and a quarter kilos), and, in the absence of an efficient interpreter and in the presence of an inquisitive crowd, it proved to be very time-consuming.

Konya did not inspire us to linger. It was just bad luck we didn't know that a

Mosque with minaret and police station in an Anatolian village. By command of Kemal Atatürk, papers were closely checked in every village, and our passage entered in our passports.

German couple lived in this remote town. We only heard this later, and were informed that we had missed a great deal by not dropping in on these kind and generous compatriots. They would certainly have shown us the famous monastery of the 'whirling dervishes,' and our impression of Konya would thus have been far better. In spite of reading up beforehand, we missed quite a few other famous

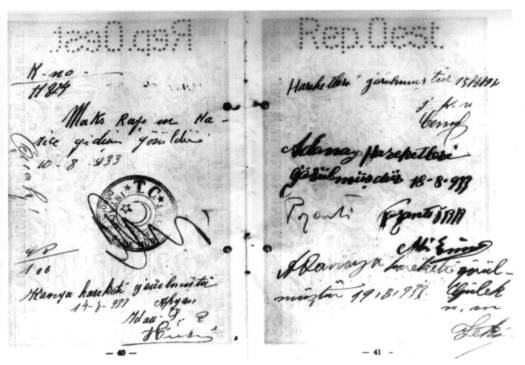

Atatürk, the father of modern Turkey, had just banned Arabic script and brought in Latin (ie Western) script. Not surprisingly, village policemen could scarcely write, and, after crossing Turkey, four pages of our passports were filled with entries like these.

landmarks along our way. Maybe we were too young to feel any special attraction to architecture or archaeology, or we were short of time, or feeling ill, or I was tinkering with the engine: there was always one reason or another.

So we left Konya that same afternoon, and darkness caught up with us on the open steppe. It was cold and we wanted to make a fire, but there was not a tree to be seen for miles; not even a weedy bit of brushwood. So, in time-honoured fashion – it was not for nothing that we had read our Karl May and Sven Hedin – we gathered dry camel and cow dung and built ourselves a beautiful stack of fuel. When it came to lighting it, we found that we had lost our matches, although we remembered from other travel accounts we had read that you could make fire by rubbing two bits of wood together. We had forgotten exactly how this was done, and anyway we hadn't any wood, so we took the sparking-plug out of the engine, put it on a petrol-soaked rag and kicked the starter a couple of times. Soon we had an excellent fire going. In spite of this, the cold got through to us at night in our little tent, and we were glad next morning when the sun began to climb in a cloudless sky.

On we went over the monotonous salt steppe. The track was scarcely visible; only a telephone wire showed us the rough direction of Karaman, our next destination.

In one tiny village, the lone policeman felt it incumbent on him to submit our passports to an especially detailed examination. He held them thoughtfully for a long time, turning them over in his hands and considering them with a mixture of curiosity and repugnance. At last we had had enough of watching his appalled expression. We took our passports out of his hand and rode on. He was really quite pleased with this way of resolving a difficult situation – he would have had to make his entries in the new-fangled Roman script, since Kemal Pasha Atatürk had outlawed Arabic – so his cries of protest were merely rhetorical.

But in the next alleyway we were brought to a halt by a completely unexpected cry. A middle-aged man was shouting at the top of his voice *"Herrgott Sakra, Deutsche! Herrgott Sakra, Deutsche!"* (Good Lord, Germans!). We got off the bike, shook his hand and introduced ourselves. He kept on repeating *"Herrgott Sakra, Deutsche!"* When we tried to get him to express his amazement at our appearance in more elaborate terms, we realised that this exclamation represented the entire extent of his German vocabulary. As he explained to us by gestures of aiming a rifle and falling down dead, accompanied by loud bang-bangs, he was indebted to the First World War for this enrichment of his linguistic capabilities. According to his performance of it, this war must have been one hilarious series of shots and tumbling over.

It is quite amazing how much one can express through gestures, and sometimes also understand. The charming thing about sign-language is that you usually think you have understood everything, but you can never be sure that you haven't got it completely wrong.

Out of all the languages whose areas we travelled through, we only spoke the few words that were important to us, for example: water, bread, where is ... ? how far ... ? and so on. It was only in Persian that we could come up with a real linguistic pearl. We were able to declare exuberantly, *"Isfahan nesfi jihan aest"* which means approximately "Isfahan is half the world." This is a very useful proverb which emphasises the splendour of old Isfahan and asserts that its wonders are worth as much to see as those of the rest of the world put together. Our conversations in Persia were a strange mixture of stammered requests for eggs, bread, or the right road, and this casually dropped observation about Isfahan.

Yet we were still in Turkey, right in the middle where the roads are nothing but the faint traces of tyre tracks and our daily distance could only be measured in the most modest terms. A few kilometres outside Eregli we came upon a camp of nomads. They had built themselves airy, tent-like shelters out of rushes and reeds under which we had a very pleasant rest during the worst of the midday heat. The friendly nomads brought us shallow bowls of gloriously cold milk and bread too; the dough seemed scarcely cooked, but it was paper-thin, half a metre in diameter and tasted superb.

More than the deep dust and sand, it was the irrigation ditches crossing our path that hindered our progress. Usually they cropped up so suddenly and the banks were so steep that the frame got caught on them and we had to level off the edges with a shovel before we could get going again. Sometimes these ditches were dry, sometimes full of water, a grey-green sluggishly flowing soup that often flooded the road for some way and mingled with the dust to form an astonishingly slippery and glutinous paste. In such places Herbert had to get off the bike and wade on ahead barefoot until he was able to make out by feel where the real ditch was and to gauge its depth. He would then give directions, "The bottom is harder here – the current's too strong over there – there's a big stone under water just in front of you," while I attempted to steer through the obstacle course. Of course we could not avoid falling over sometimes and soon all three of us – the machine, Herbert and I – were plastered with a crust of dried grey mud. We could not have wished for better protective colouring. Every spot of white paint, every shiny bit of metal was camouflaged against the background of the steppe, but the area was so safe and free of bandits that this protection was unnecessary.

The gradient of the plateau continued to rise. In front of us we saw a mountain railway, the Taurus, that reminded us of the Alps. We crossed the Taurus track, and, at Ulukisla, at a height of 1400 metres, we reached the top of the pass. Then came a steep descent southwards on a pretty good road which curved about boldly through rocks bare of vegetation, with the Mediterranean glinting in the distance. We came down fast and passed though the famous Cilician Gate through which Alexander the Great, the Caliph Haroun al Rashid, the Romans and the Crusaders had travelled before us.

The midday heat was different here from on the Anatolian steppe, where it was dry and had a rather subtle character. In the shade of a rock or a tent it was always cool, and heat depended on the rays of the sun. Here it was in the very air, leaden and enervating, pursuing us even into the narrowest and shadiest gorge. A mountain torrent dashing down over the rocks looked inviting for a dip. What a disappointment! The water that looked as cool as if it were welling up from a great spring or off the edge of a glacier was in fact the temperature of a bath which you've just run steaming hot from the tap, but which you've been prevented from enjoying straightaway because the telephone rang. So we sat there in a lukewarm shower bath and sweated. Then we dipped our shirts in the water and put them on wet. The evaporation as we rode on gave us a cool feeling for a little while at least.

Down and down we went. At Pozanti we were still at a height of 780 metres. Now the area became quite European. Among conifer forests and steep rock walls which would have gladdened the heart of any mountaineer we felt as if we'd been transported to the Dolomites. Even the people here looked European once more. The old-fashioned costumes of the nomads with their gorgeous colours were left behind. Here the sports cap was preferred – not the elegant English model, alas, but a rather dowdy old style.

I switched off the engine and we freewheeled down into the valley in the gathering dusk. As the high rock walls glowed even more red in the setting sun and thousands of cicadas chirped their farewells, we pitched our tent on the edge of the plain.

The next morning we tasted luscious grapes in Tarsus, and by midday we were in Adana. To the north, the Taurus mountains towered against the sky, to the south lay the blue Mediterranean – a glorious position for a city.

Only a hundred kilometres more lay between us and Syria. Another passport check, the last Turkish one. We were almost emotional as we allowed the ceremony to wash over us. It was the end of a protracted torture. Six pages of our passports were covered with the childlike scrawls of Turkish policemen. If you crossed Turkey by land four times, you would have to apply for a new passport. But maybe officials will become less enthusiastic about making entries once the novelty of using European script has worn off. Adieu, Turkey!

# 4
# JOY AND WOE IN PARADISE

The Syrians greeted us in fluent French on their side of the border. At least, it seemed fluent to us, but then our command of the language was most inadequate. In fact we were not equipped with any particular language skills for our journey. On my return, people so often asked, "I suppose you speak ever so many languages, don't you?" What I usually did was to nod my head and murmur. Yes, languages were a precondition for any journey, but now at last I can confess the truth, and Herbert will not hold it against me. Between the two of us we could only speak one language properly, and that was German. Even in that we were a bit specialised. In moments of excitement I would frequently fall back into Tyrolese, while Herbert regularly used Viennese words which I had never heard in Kufstein. In the end, when we found ourselves staying in the Himalaya with the family of a forester from North Germany, we had a lot of difficulty making ourselves immediately understandable to one another. Talk about everyday things went rattling on, of course, and it was usually Mother Johanssen who brought to our attention the differences between German dialects.

"What do you want to eat today?" she asked.

"*An' Sterz!*" I cried

"*Palatschinken*," requested Herbert.

Mother Johanssen gave us a helpless look and then said decisively, "Today it's *Pfannkuchen* (pancakes)." And this, of course, was what we had both been asking for!

Apart from German, it was Herbert who knew more English and I who knew more French – just about enough to carry on a polite, superficial conversation. As for the languages of other countries, we always managed to pick up the few necessary words as we went along. You really don't have to be a linguistic genius if all you want is a smooth trouble-free journey. I once heard of a language researcher who had so many difficulties with the police in Turkey that in the end he had to flee the country.

A little human understanding, no arrogance, and especially not the assumption that you are dealing with 'natives' – all this helps. A cheerful smile sometimes does more than a perfectly turned sentence.

So it may be that the Syrians' French was not as good as it appeared to us, but the roads were even better than we had hoped in our wildest dreams. They were glorious smooth ribbons of tarmac on which we simply ate up the kilometres. Of course, it was a blissful feeling, being really able to open up and go at last, but there were disadvantages. All those small local details that we had been able to observe so closely at our snail's pace though Turkey now flew past us unseen.

Iskanderun or Alexandretta was a bewitching little town with all the charm of the eastern Mediterranean: Arabs in the streets, many still wearing the *burnous* as a reminder of the desert, but many in modern European suits with ties in colours of glowing splendour that would have shocked a Van Gogh. There were many new buildings too – villas such as might have been seen in the finer suburbs of Paris before the Great War, and ultra-modern Cubist buildings with huge windows, in fact, a thoroughly pleasing mixture of Asia and Europe, or rather, of Arabia and Paris.

It seemed to us that French culture was deeply rooted here, and after travelling for a whole week through Asia Minor, we were surprised to find that Europe was still strong so far into Asia. Then we remembered that the town had been founded by Alexander the Great and that it bore his name. We were bound to come across traces of his passing all the way to India, indeed, even in India many statues of the Buddha have Greek rather than Asian facial characteristics. Our esteem for the achievements of modern Europe wilted, and also the esteem we felt for our own enterprise.

In a few hours on good roads we covered the distance from Alexandretta to Aleppo. The town has a mediaeval aspect, with a massive ruined castle towering over it. It reminded us of the Crusades when the Crescent fought the Cross here. We were sorry that we had forgotten so many details from our history lessons. Our journey here was like leafing through a living history book: here a name would take us back to Greek times, outside this town Richard the Lionheart had stood, and here again Persians had threatened to push Europe back from the Mediterranean.

Originally we had intended to stay only a few hours in Aleppo, long enough to overhaul the motorcycle and have a stroll round the town. However, this turned into five days, because of the tremendous heat. As a result, we were unable to do anything except lie on the beds in our bare hotel room like dead men and gulp down ice-cold fluids. We had raging headaches, and could not sleep at night. Eventually we summoned a doctor whose laconic pronouncement was "Sunstroke!" We therefore bought ourselves a couple of pith helmets, which at that time were to be found all over the Near East. Today they have completely disappeared. Have people become more resistant to heat, or what? We finally completed the small repairs to our machine and, in the afternoon of 23rd August 1933, just as the shadow of the castle was creeping down over the town, we rode out into the desert. The road ran straight as a die and disappeared on the horizon without the least hint of a bend. To avoid the heat we rode late into the night, but even then the air was unchanged and buffeted our ears like a hot *Föhn*. It was a strange and unfamiliar contrast – the dark night and the heat making us sweat – and when at last we lay down to sleep in the desert, the sand was as hot as if it were being heated from underneath.

Even before dawn the next day the temperature was already at a ferociously high level and the glowing red ball of the sun gave us the impression of some dreadful scourge. We made ourselves face-masks out of linen which we wore under the front of our tropical helmets, hanging down to our chests, with big round holes cut out only for the eyes. Short trousers and sleeveless shirts also proved an agony in the midday heat. Long trousers and long sleeves would have kept off the heat better.

The well of Ain Aroos, where Rebekah met Isaac, lies 5km south of the border between Turkey and Syria at Tel Abiad.

Seeing the Bedouin going about muffled up to their noses like skiers in a snowstorm, we realised that 'warm' clothing, especially wool, gives protection against heat as well as against cold. That's why in the heat one should put clothes *on* rather than take them *off*, but we were not yet wise to these desert tricks.

Our best moments came when we immersed ourselves fully clothed in the muddy water of a canal or the Euphrates and went on our way dripping wet. In a few minutes the hot breeze dried our clothes completely, but these few minutes were heavenly and we were always on the look out for possible 'soaks,' as we called them. With our masks and dripping clothing we must have presented a strange spectacle, riding like ghosts through the shimmering heat of the landscape.

When we arrived at the Euphrates, flowing sluggishly through the desert, we thought immediately how dirty it was. Although we were thirsty we did not drink its water. In spite of all our inoculations, we thought inevitably of cholera, typhus, plague and smallpox. We were not very clear about how these diseases were transmitted, so we were highly suspicious of the brown waters of the Euphrates, and we rode along beside the river in the searing heat of Mesopotamia in August with nothing to drink. Sometimes, as described, we stopped for a short dip, just to cool off, but could not avoid getting water on our faces and round our mouths. These were very bad moments, but we held out. At last we came to a little settlement and I said in my best Arabic. "*Mai, mai* – water, water," and they brought us an earthenware jug of lovely cool water. These clay jugs are a wonderful invention and do the job of a refrigerator –

well, almost. Clay is porous and water penetrates to the outer surface of the jug where it evaporates and cools what remains inside. The water we drank seemed ice cold to us. It can't have been much colder than a cup of lukewarm tea, but nevertheless represented a record low, seeing that the air temperature was around 40°C and every metal part on our motorcycle was so hot that we burned our fingers on it. It's only on a journey like this that you begin to understand how everything is relative.

So there we sat on the banks of the Euphrates, congratulating ourselves for having avoided its disease-laden water, and drank and drank.

"Was that difficult?" I asked Herbert.

He understood immediately what I meant.

"No," he said, but I could tell at once that he was lying, "I would never think of drinking from the Euphrates. I want to get to India!"

"Of course," I said, "we'd be fools to give ourselves dysentery at this stage."

I don't know why I suddenly thought of dysentery, but the soupy grey Euphrates suddenly brought it to mind. Then we held out our jugs again and made gestures to the hospitable peasants, "*Mai, mai.*" They laughed to show they had understood and ran off to the Euphrates – where else? There they filled the jugs with fresh dirty water which they solemnly offered us.

After that we always drank straight from the Euphrates. Everything's relative, as I said. Only once did we go thirsty all day, and that was when we saw a dead bloated camel go sailing by. This was where we drew the line on relativity.

Our desert journey was to take us to Baghdad, city of the caliph Haroun al Rashid. A strong wind had got up, blowing dust and sand clouds in our faces, but it did not cool us at all. Here and there the storm had swept the sand off the rocky ground. We had to ride around individual blocks of stone and whole piles of scree. In other places the wheels stuck fast in deep sand dunes and it took all the power of the engine plus our own energetic efforts to get free again. A skilled pillion rider is crucial at such moments. My good friend Herbert, who sat behind me for the whole thirteen thousand kilometre journey, soon became expert at judging the state of the running surface. It is an error to think of the pillion rider solely as a passenger. Much depends on him and on his state of alertness. Just like the man in front, he has to be constantly aware of the state of the ground. He must know by the sound of the engine how hard the machine is working in the sand, and whether it is going to make it or is liable to get stuck. The main thing when riding through sand is to keep up the momentum. The watchword is "Don't stop!"

Whenever Herbert noticed that the engine was straining at its last gasp, he would nip off behind and get pushing. He did it so neatly that I often didn't notice that he was no longer on the motorcycle. This resulted in half comic, half tragic situations. When the surface eventually grew better and I chanced to turn round for a quick word with Herbert, he would have disappeared! This meant that the good chap had been left standing far behind in the desert, sometimes many kilometres back, all alone and callously abandoned by his friend. As far as road conditions allowed, I would ride back, but Herbert had many a long walk through the desert. Then he would begin to revolt and say, "Why don't you let me have a go up in front for once? Then you can see how you like pushing and being left behind and having to traipse along on foot ..."

The mighty citadel of Aleppo in Syria. The Crusaders never succeeded in capturing Damascus or Aleppo, so the Christian Kingdom of Jerusalem and the pilgrim route to the Holy Land were always under threat from these two Islamic strongpoints. If Damascus and Aleppo had fallen into Christian hands, then the Syrian desert would have become a no-man's land several hundred kilometres wide between Islam and Christendom. Christian Palestine might have lasted not just 88 years but maybe to the present day.

So we would sometimes try riding lessons in the desert, but it was really quite impossible to learn how to ride a motorcycle on our 'pantechnicon.' Thus it was that I remained up front all the way to India.

Looking back, I can't say who contributed more to the expedition, the driver or the pillion passenger. Apart from pushing and being left behind, Herbert had other sufferings to endure. Just imagine: we had only got as far as Anatolia when the spring in his saddle broke. This pillion saddle was the best that could be had in those days, a so-called 'suspension saddle,' tailored to a person's weight and to different road conditions. This miraculous construction had only one disadvantage: its spring was a strangely complicated curlicue of steel that no village blacksmith in Europe or Asia was capable of reproducing. We telegraphed straight away to Vienna from Turkey to have one sent to Baghdad for us. Whenever Herbert began to complain that he was getting corns in the most unusual parts of the body, I would console him by saying, "Patience! It's only nine hundred more kilometres to Baghdad and then we get the new spring."

This was not how it turned out, and the story of this spring is worth a short mention. At the Consulate in Baghdad there was no sign of the eagerly awaited spring. We sent another wire to Vienna, but after all, we couldn't wait in Baghdad for ever, so we left directions for the spring to be sent to Teheran and rode on our way to Persia. When we eventually reached Teheran, there was still no spring. It had gone missing: a curse upon the customs official somewhere who would not let it through. Cursing was not much help to poor Herbert, but he got used to the hard seat and rode all the way to India on it.

We didn't need the spring any more and erased the whole thing from our minds. We came back to Europe and neither Herbert nor I thought any more about it. But that was not the end of the affair. When I got back to Baghdad two years later in the course of my journey round the world in the Steyr 100 – two years later, mark you – the Consulate informed me that as well as my letters there was a parcel for me. A parcel? Great stuff – I wasn't expecting one, but I guessed some friends back in the Tyrol were sending me Austrian cigarettes or some other little surprise. Full of pleasant expectation, I asked, "So where is my parcel, please?" The consular secretary – he was the same one as two years before – brought me the little wooden box and said with a smile, "It's been lying here quite a while and run up a few transport charges. That'll be two Iraqi pounds and seven hundred *fils*."

I still didn't suspect anything. "Just give me the parcel." I paid over the considerable sum and received my parcel. Inside was the spring for Herbert's saddle! On our bike trip in 1933 we had been longing for this spare part as the most precious gift heaven could send. Two years later, here it lay in my hands, totally worthless. I manifested complete unconcern to the Consulate and withdrew in a dignified manner, taking my historic parcel with me. From the terrace of the Tigris Palace Hotel I wrote a letter to Herbert in Vienna, "Guess what turned up in Baghdad today ... ?" Then I solemnly committed the saddle spring to the waters of the Tigris

On the journey through the once-green paradise between the Tigris and Euphrates it was so hot that we wore ghostly-looking face-masks to protect us from the sand and heat. Carping critics back home had insisted that it was madness to ride deliberately through the desert in August. They were right, but on a six month journey across half of Asia, problems with the climate are inescapable. For example, if we had set off later, then we would have arrived in India in the ghastly confusion of the monsoon rains.

But on with the story of our motorcycle trip to India. We were on our way from Aleppo to Baghdad. For a number of days, nothing much interesting happened along the way, until in the sandy and stony plain we came upon some ruins. With the help of our good English maps we worked out that it must be the ancient Assyrian city of Doura. One year previously, Americans had dug here and made off back across the ocean with some valuable finds. We rested in the shade of a ruined wall and I fetched the writing things from the big carrying-case strapped on over the tank. It was a lot of effort to keep a daily log of all the technical data and observations about how the machine was performing. Alongside this, I also had to get down on paper all the usual travel impressions and notes for press articles. As I took out my writing case and the log book, I noticed that something of mine was missing, something very important that could scupper the entire trip, or at least put a brake on it: my passport had gone! I searched everywhere, turned out the entire case, but in vain. The passport had disappeared.

This appalling realisation made me go hot all over, in spite of the Syrian summer heat. Without a passport it was impossible to cross the Iraqi border. That could mean months of waiting while officials argued over my fate. The consequences of the situation were unthinkable. Not only did my passport contain an Iraqi visa, but also a Persian, an Afghan and an Indian one. If you have any idea of the trouble it costs to acquire such unusual visas – the consular negotiations, the hopes and the fears – then you will be able to gauge my state of mind as I sat on the sand with no passport in the ruined city of Doura.

Near Aleppo we saw these peculiar 'beehive villages.' Wood is scarce, so roofs are built out of mud in dome shapes like this, rather than flat.

Northern Syria: strict Moslem wearing baggy trousers. The great Prophet Mohammed will be born into the world a second time, but shall that great honour fall to a woman again? In all fairness, Allah will surely bestow this great honour on a man. As it cannot be known when that will be or who will be chosen, and as men are inexperienced in such matters, they wear these baggy trousers, 'just in case,' so that the child Mohammed will not fall too hard upon the earth.

Where was this well-nigh irreplaceable document? We had fallen off once that day and the machine had rolled over in the sand. Could the case on the tank have sprung open and the passport fallen out? It was certainly a possibility.

Then, further along the way we had come upon a particularly well-bleached camel skeleton. We had photographed it and fooled around with it. We had put the front half of the skeleton up on the bike and taken pictures of that too. Then we put a sun helmet on the skull and subjected the poor creature to all sorts of other indignities.

Youthful high spirits usually get their come-uppance (I was only twenty years old then, which may be some mitigation), and this was our reward. The passport had probably fallen out when we took the cameras out of the big case without paying attention. Now it was lying somewhere in the desert, probably already gone with the wind and buried under sand dunes.

I felt such a complete idiot – what sort of dressing-down would I get from the worthy directors of Puch when they saw me wheeled home in disgrace?

"All that money spent on an expedition to India and then the boy goes and loses his passport in the desert!" It didn't bear thinking about.

I made up my mind to retrace our exact route and search the whole way we had come. Herbert stayed behind in Doura. The Americans had left a little bungalow which had been used during their research, and Herbert installed himself in it. With a few tins of food, a stack of Arab flatbread, a bag of dates and one of the two five-litre water carriers, he was set up for the next few days.

I can't remember now why we decided to separate at this juncture. I believe we each wanted to be alone for a while. On an expedition like this, all sorts of unspoken tensions inevitably build up, even between close friends. The pressures of climate and physical exertion make great demands on the nervous system. Then there are the small clashes of personality caused by living exclusively in each other's company for months at a time, with no break or variety.

Whatever the case, I went back alone, in the forlorn hope of finding the passport and intending to go through the oasis of Mayadin and thence to Dayr-az-Zawr. There was a telegraph office there and I would be able to communicate with the Austrian Consul in Damascus. Then it would be up to the authorities to puzzle over my fate. Probably this would be a slow process and I would have to wait and wait and wait until a decision came down the wires between Vienna and Damascus. This loss of time could well mean that we would arrive in India amid the downpours and floods of the monsoon. The consequences of my carelessness were incalculable. How was it possible to lose my passport? Why not my own head?

Such were my thoughts of overwhelming remorse and repentance as I climbed aboard the innocent and unsuspecting Puch and rode it back the same way we had come. The wind was still strong, and the further I rode, the harder I found it to follow our tracks. I managed to find the place where we had played our rude games with the skeleton, but I did not find the passport, so on I went. I searched in vain at the place where we had fallen off – probably I had already passed it too far to the east – so I went on towards Mayadin and Dayr-az-Zawr. Once I stopped to take a sip of water, but the feeling of thirst never goes away and lips that are chapped by sand seem to burn worse the more you moisten them. I was perhaps one or two hours from Mayadin when I noticed, far off on the horizon, a dark spot wreathed in a little cloud of dust. Soon I made out a lone rider hurtling through the desert on a white racing camel. The magnificent animal came bounding in my direction with grotesque loping strides and the rider soon came to a halt in front of me. I switched off my engine as the camel sank to its knees with the dignified and laborious movements of the ship of the desert. The rider approached me and spoke my name inquiringly. Then the man reached into the fathomless depths of his full white *galabiya* and, with that calmly ceremonious air which only the Oriental possesses, what should he hand over to me but *my passport!* My dearly beloved, deeply regretted passport!

What poet could have described my joy as everything was explained. My passport had been found in the caravanserai at Mayadin and the local mayor had sent a man on a racing camel after us. We had spent the night there and taken a few photographs the next morning, which was when the passport had probably slipped out of the open case over the tank. The camel rider asked whether he could have the pictures we had taken in Mayadin. I doubt if he'll ever get them. Time and again on trips through Asia we would try to explain to people that we weren't like promenade photographers who could let them have their snaps five minutes later, but to anyone travelling in those parts in the future, I would strongly recommend taking that sort of camera. These people are basically so good-natured that to be able to take someone's picture and give them a print straightaway would really open their hearts. In the end, my camel rider was very content with a decent *baksheesh* and we parted with many *salaams*.

Herbert was in sombre mood when I found him again in the ruins of Doura. He had been writing a few letters to send home at the next opportunity. However, as soon as he saw me joyfully brandishing my passport, everything was better, and even the unaccountable tensions that had hovered between us in recent days seemed to have been blown away.

The day after next we reached Abu Kemal, a crucial military base in the Syrian desert. Here we met with the French Lieutenant Etienne Cabane, our first European since Istanbul. This officer had, with exquisite taste, made a home for himself in an Arab house. It must have cost a deal of trouble and money to bring all the items from France to Syria and to install them. There was a private distillation plant for filtering water from the Euphrates to make it drinkable and a good clean kitchen with a store of tins containing every sort of food to delight a discriminating French palate. On the roof terrace we spent a very merry evening. Countless aperitifs disappeared down our dried-out throats and oiled the conversation, which went back and forth in a lively way. Lieutenant Cabane told us about the lonely life he led and about how he longed for Paris where his young wife had been waiting a year now for his return. The French government would not allow her to share his lonely existence in this dangerous frontline post.

Then he explained to us that only thirteen days previously there had been bitter fighting with Bedouin insurgents which had claimed seven hundred lives. Lieutenant Cabane observed unemotionally that, had we arrived in the area a fortnight earlier, we would have made it seven hundred and two.

It is a relief to hear these things *after* the event. In August 1933 the newspapers in Europe were filled every day with reports of this Bedouin revolt. Our friends, knowing that we were in the area, were extremely anxious and prepared themselves for the worst. Meanwhile we, in our youthful romantic frenzy, were sailing through the desert without a care, in total ignorance of the cruel and bloody battles taking place a few hundred kilometres to the south. There's nothing like a nice quiet

In Abu Kemal, the oasis on the border between Syria and Iraq, we stop outside the house of the hospitable Etienne Cabane. This oasis was an important military base in the fight against the rebels of the Bedouin revolt.

journey, well away from telegrams and newspapers. The fact that this often causes terrible anxiety to those left at home is another story altogether.

We only became fully aware of the seriousness of the situation at the end of our stay at Lieutenant Cabane's. Beside the little Puch motorcycle loomed a mighty armoured car with swivelling machine guns and a crew of French colonial soldiers. Lieutenant Cabane escorted us himself.

This was a fine thing. Whenever we got stuck, the soldiers leapt out of the car and pushed with all their might. Several times they wanted to load our cycle on to their four-wheel-drive desert vehicle, but we refused with dignity. In the last rays of the setting sun, after a journey of eleven hours, we reached the border of Syria and Mesopotamia. A single stone marking the border stood on a sandhill, announcing in Arabic script that we were now entering biblical Mesopotamia, known today as Iraq. Lieutenant Cabane shook us by the hand. Here was where his authority ended. The vehicle turned and soon disappeared between the sand dunes and rocky hills of the Syrian desert.

Iraq is a modern country. In spite of the fact that no motorcycle before us had entered the biblical land of rivers by the desert route, the customs officer at the little border fort behaved as if it were an everyday occurrence. I warmed to such people. I sang his praises and surreptitiously helped him to stamp the page in the right place. His dignity was preserved and our way was smoothed, the main advantage being that I had back my lost passport! I revelled in the knowledge that my papers were in order.

We did not reach the next desert fort until early evening. The garrison, regarding us as a pleasant diversion from the desperate monotony of their duties, insisted on our staying overnight. They kept on giving us big clumps of sweet sticky dates, cool jugs of water – we knew it came out of the Euphrates – and flatbread. The hospitality of these rough fighting men was touching, but we rode on nevertheless. Even in the moonlight the road tracks were clearly recognisable and we wanted to put a few kilometres behind us without having to suffer under the sun's rays. Besides this, our hearts were set on actually sleeping in the desert. Night in the desert is overwhelmingly beautiful, and can be described only with difficulty.

We stopped just where we were. The last explosions of the engine died away and an uncanny silence descended, but soon we got used to the lack of sound and enjoyed it. The ground was dry and we laid our sleeping bags in a hollow in the sand. A thin linen sheet was the only covering needed, not so much as a protection against cold as against venomous insects. Then we lay still. The sky was a gigantic hemisphere above us, the stars were brighter and more radiant than at home and the moon was almost painfully white. The silence was so complete that we could almost hear it – paradoxical, but true.

Our route took us mainly along the Euphrates – a river through the desert, but a desert that was once a paradise of fertile fields and flourishing gardens and which today is still a paradise for archaeologists.

Assyrians, Babylonians, Medes, Persians – all came and held sway, then disappeared. After them came the Greeks, the Romans, the Turks, and the British. Even the Germans ventured into the land between the rivers, but all of them retreated again from this harsh theatre of history and the two rivers continued to flow undisturbed from the wild rocky mountains of Anatolia all the way to the Persian Gulf.

Every day, when the noontide heat became overpowering and we found no village to give us shade, we would take refuge in the inviting waters of the Euphrates. Immersed up to the neck in muddy soup, with sun helmets on our heads, we let the sluggish river and the sluggish hours ripple by us.

Here we made the acquaintance of other travellers on their way downstream like ourselves. Their destination was either Baghdad or the ancient city of Karbala. One fine day, somewhere in the upper reaches of the Euphrates in the wilds of Kurdistan, they would leave their poor huts and pack for the journey. A few small possessions and the voluminous robes that take up so little space when folded would be stuffed into a watertight bag made of ram's leather. The bag was then blown up very hard and the ends fastened tightly. Then Ahmed and Abdullah would enter the water stark naked, clasp both arms around their bundle which at the same time did duty as water-wings, and allow themselves to drift down with the current. They would kick their legs occasionally, but more because they felt like it than to hasten their journey. This strange progress would last many weeks, as they stopped off many times to be given food and shelter by fellow tribesmen.

On one occasion I accompanied one of these floating Arabs a short way downstream and I must say that later, when we got back on the motorbike and were riding through the burning desert, I thoroughly envied his pleasant and comfortable way of travelling. We both held tight to the swimbag in which I had been invited to stow my shirt and shorts, and we drifted slowly by the monotonous landscape of

Ahmed has stowed his belongings in a watertight leather bag.

the river banks, past high water wheels which creaked and groaned, raising jar after jar of Euphrates water high in the air and tipping it into a channel where it flowed through the fields, conjuring a green paradise out of the grey desert.

From a lone tent on the bank came a cry in Arabic to us swimmers, an invitation to lunch, as my companion explained. Soon we were seated in the tent, (still stark naked, for there were no ladies present), and were being plied with raw cucumber, dates and black coffee. It seemed to be a matter of course to entertain pilgrims without charge and even my offer of payment was rejected with indignation.

As I took leave of my Arab friend to trek back to our motorcycle, he looked after me, considering me with amazement. He was very likely thinking that foreigners must be pretty daft to struggle on like that under the hot Arabian sun over dusty roads, when they could just as well make the same journey at no cost while bathing in the gentle refreshing water, which would get them to the same place in the end, *inshallah*, God willing.

We continued our motorcycle journey with a little less self-confidence, but then we consoled ourselves with the thought that while Ahmed and Abdullah were still floating down the Euphrates, we would be in India. If we had tried this argument on Ahmed, he would probably have replied, "But we don't want to go to India, just to Karbala!" In which he would have been perfectly right.

The caravan path along the Euphrates was not much used but towards evening on the 29th August, we came across many tyre tracks in the sand. These branched out more and more and after a while huge vehicles appeared on the horizon, all full of

Europeans. We seemed to be approaching a town that we were quite unable to find on the map. A signboard told us it was Hadithah. It had mushroomed within a few weeks, an eloquent symbol of British enterprise.

The Kirkuk-Haifa oil pipeline, then under construction, crosses the Euphrates at this point. Full of wonder and amazement, we were looking at a technical feat of gigantic proportions. A pipeline a thousand kilometres long was being laid straight across the desert. Just keeping the countless workers and engineers on the different construction sites supplied with food and water posed a problem that could scarcely be imagined in a European context.

In Hadithah the pipes were loaded on to lorries and driven direct by night and by day to the outlying construction sites, which might be up to five hundred kilometres away. These trucks had been specially built for the job by an American company. They were articulated lorries with five axles, of which three were power-driven. The load-bearing capacity of these desert giants was *sixty* tonnes! The pipes did not weigh so much in themselves, but water for drinking and building needs was transported in them at the same time. Here we reported to Mr Roggers, the all-powerful boss of this building section. Our letter of recommendation from the Shell offices in Vienna was not lacking in effect.

Every evening we sat in the dining room of a corrugated iron bungalow at tables with white cloths and dined with the British. Gigantic fans whirled in a ghostly way overhead and Arab servants in picturesque costumes silently brought in one course after another. All the dishes were selected for the desert climate: roast chicken, delicate vegetables, custards, vanilla ice cream and fruit. If it had not been for the dust of the desert which hung in the air and which could even be felt in the food between one's teeth, it was almost like being somewhere in Europe.

Besides, the British were renowned sports enthusiasts and although it was a Saturday night they raised no objection to our not appearing in dinner jackets. These did not form part of our extensive and yet modest equipment for the motorcycle trip, but our immaculate lightweight plus-four suits were perfectly decent, and that was the main thing. Later in our journey, we caused a sensation with these excellent garments in Teheran and a revolution in Persian fashion. I'll explain later how that came about.

We were very comfortable with the British in Hadithah, had our shirts washed at the laundry and our socks darned. We had already done this a few times ourselves, but I never took any pleasure in that sort of activity. Herbert got himself a haircut from the oil-town barber. I was glad about this, as it reduced the effect of the chopping I had inflicted on his head with an 'expedition cut' in Anatolia.

In other words, we restored ourselves and began to look quite presentable again. This life of luxury in the desert was very much to our liking, and we were not at all displeased when a sandstorm blew up and we were told that it was impossible for us to continue. The howling of the storm was really most alarming. Thick swathes of sand and dust swept past the windows of our corrugated iron hut with terrific force. Heaven and earth merged into the same grey colour and the sun was completely invisible. For two days we remained safely in the shelter of Hadithah, and did nothing but eat well, lie on comfortable camp beds and read English newspapers. We also wrote a whole lot of letters home.

In 1933 the Iraq Petroleum Company laid a pipeline diagonally across the Arabian Desert. We arrived in Haditha just in time to witness the construction of this 1,000 km long oil pipe between Kirkuk and Haifa. We also saw how the engineers were opening up new wells and generously giving water to the Bedouin and their herds. It was the dawn of a new era of mechanisation in the desert.

Meeting a caravan in a sandstorm between Dayr-az-Zawr and Hit.

Cars armed with machine-guns belonging to British-Iraqi troops in the Syrian desert.
We rode unmolested and in total innocence through the desert, while in the summer
of 1933 a Bedouin revolt raged, leaving 700 dead.

Finally, however, we got bored with doing nothing. We had got our strength up
again and longed to be back in the saddle of our machine. The storm had lost some of
its ferocity, but it was still extremely unpleasant as we packed up the Puch once more
and rode to the oil-town filling station. It was the strangest petrol station I had ever
seen. There was nothing but a pipe coming out of the ground with a tap and a hose.

"Help yourself," said one of the British engineers, so we unscrewed the pipe and
filled the Puch's belly. We could take on board 40 litres of petrol altogether.

We had scarcely left the last workmen's huts of Hadithah behind us than we
became aware that the storm was still too fierce for the safety of our two-wheeled
vehicle. Things had not looked so bad from the window of the cosy bungalow.

It took all the power of the machine and my sense of balance to brace ourselves
against the violent squalls that came at us sideways and several times forced us to
the ground. Sand got into our clothes, mouths and noses and behind our goggles. It
was a most unpleasant ride.

We struggled on for eighty kilometres to the oasis of Hit, in the course of which we
frequently lost our way and, because of poor visibility, made several long detours. In
Hit we stayed overnight in a miserable caravanserai and were thoroughly unhappy
with our wretched surroundings. After abandoning ourselves to luxury with the
British in Hadithah, we were bound to be discontented. There is nothing harder to
bear than a run of good days ...

The following day, to our enormous relief, the storm dropped, and high time too,
for our eyes were sticky with sand and sweat, and our bodies in torment from the
thousand pinpricks of lashing grains of sand.

Woven baskets serve as transport on the Euphrates.

Our clothes were heavy as lead with huge deposits of sand in every pocket and fold. I had burned my left leg badly when the exhaust pipe came down on top of me in a crash. Because the machine was so heavy, it had needed all Herbert's help to get me free again.

But these are only details. We were young and had a great goal before us, the sort that many young people dream of, but few ever achieve. Whether we would succeed was still in question, but at least we were on our way.

It was such a beautiful world that opened up before us, and the desert, so often represented as boring, made a tremendous impression. There's one unusually beautiful and deeply moving image that remains in my mind from the journey to Baghdad. A few Arab gravestones stood in the midst of an endless expanse, with a saddled horse standing nearby. In the rays of the setting sun, an Arab dressed all in white cast himself upon the sand, touching the ground with his forehead and rising again, softly chanting his *surah*. He was praying to the One God of the desert, and we foreigners were unworthy of his attention.

This melancholy vision stayed with us a long time, while the soft, long-drawn-out chanting of the *surah* rang in our ears. We went on our way through the desert in pensive mood, without a word to say.

We wanted to make up for the time we had spent in Hadithah, which had been a bit of a waste, however pleasant, and so we decided to ride on through the night. In the light of the headlamp, the tracks in the sand showed up in relief. Frightened gazelles fled away from it, and, in the distance, we heard the long drawn shriek of a hyena.

In the light of the southern full moon, night was as bright as day, and this soon made our headlamp unnecessary. The sky was sprinkled with millions of stars whose brilliance was beyond compare with that of our home latitudes.

Not until well after midnight did we make a halt and put up our tropical tent. This took next to no time, but blowing up the air mattresses left us gasping and cursing. Later we were relieved of this torture in Baluchistan where we had red ants of quite intimidating size, and their acid made thousands of holes in the beds, so that they leaked. After that we threw them away and slept on the bare earth.

In the meantime we still had the airbeds and prepared to sleep in comfort. Then we made a meal of the last of the sandwiches the British had provided us with and opened two cans of beer. We were all right for the time being. However, these were the last of our British delights and we had no idea what we would do for the next day's meal. The question of food bothered us very little on the entire journey. We were unable to carry more provisions because of lack of space, so we always ate what fate put in our way. One day it would be fit for a king, the next it would be very simple, and often it was not very appetising. Wherever we could we drank tea or coffee and devoured a vast number of watermelons, which are available in every oasis from Anatolia to India. Of course, these irregular feasts occasionally had consequences that even large doses of animal charcoal could not assuage. Then what usually happened was that, after riding no more than a kilometre, Herbert would urgently shout, "Stop!" or else I would suddenly bring the machine to a halt with the same compulsion. It was a good thing that we were not usually smitten at the same moment, as someone had to hold the machine while the other rushed out into the desert in order to disappear into the (non-existent) bushes. These were what you might call the minor inconveniences of a long trip.

I once suggested the following topic for debate : suppose you are travelling through the desert with a girl – an absolutely flat desert, that is – and furthermore, let's suppose that she's the sort of girl who always gets terribly embarrassed and doesn't trust you to look the other way.

We discussed the problem for some considerable time and finally hit on a simple geographical solution: all the girl has to do is walk eight kilometres out into the desert. Then, when she squats down, only her head will be visible, *because of the curve of the Earth* ...

# BAGHDAD – IN THE FOOTSTEPS OF HAROUN AL RASHID

We were awakened by the shuffling of camels' feet. Two riders on racing camels stood by our camp in the moonlight. How on earth had they located us in the flat open desert? We had deliberately ridden some way off the main track, too. They were Iraqi soldiers, clad in gorgeous colours, heavily armed with rifles and revolvers, with cartridge belts crossed over their chests. The camels in colourful harness made repulsive bleating noises at us and showed their yellow teeth. The two soldiers, one an Arab and the other a Negro, cut immaculate if somewhat rakish figures. They asked us, "Who, why, where to ... ?" Our answer, namely "Two Austrian students going to India on a motorcycle" didn't seem to mean much to them, but anyway, they evidently did not consider that our presence in the desert represented a danger to the Iraqi state. With a dignified, "Allah go with you!" they remounted their camels and sped away into the black nothingness.

The next day, too, we met numerous military patrols on camels and with cross-country desert vehicles equipped with machine guns. There were fears that the Bedouin uprising might spill over into Iraq. Another two days' journey brought us within sight of Baghdad, the first big staging post of this long journey, and one which we dearly wished to see. We got the ferry across the Euphrates at Fallujah and were then in the real between-rivers-land, the country between the Euphrates and the Tigris. In Arabic It is called 'the Jesireh' roughly meaning 'island.'

The traffic on the road and alongside it grew busier, and here we met with camel and donkey caravans, horse-drawn wagons, and more and more cars. We crossed over the Tigris on a shaky pontoon bridge where some oriental edifice, towering as in a dream, was silhouetted against a glassy sky. We shouted to each other in delight as the machine went along, singing student songs out of sheer high spirits. We were beside ourselves with joy and wild with happiness. It was no longer just a dream; nor were we being deluded by a mirage: we were actually arriving at the fairytale city of Baghdad, the city of Haroun al Rashid! The towers and minarets twinkled and shone in the light of the setting sun.

When I was still a very little boy I had a burning desire to know the Orient. With cheeks aglow I read the travel stories of Pierre Loti and Karl May, and dreamed of visiting Baghdad, 'that most oriental of all cities.' I pictured it to myself in detail: I would approach the city at the head of a richly-decked caravan, the onion domes

Once, Iraqi desert police on camels discovered our bivouac in the early morning, just as we were packing up the tent. Who were we? Where were we going on this strange form of transport in the middle of the desert? Could we be hashish smugglers? Every time we had to answer a lot of questions.

of the mosques would be gleaming in the setting sun, and, from a minaret the muezzin would be calling aloud the summons to prayer.

Now the dream of my youth was about to come true. No matter that the caravan of my dreams had had to give way to motor transport which brought me in comfort, but above all more quickly across the flat desert. Suddenly the tyre tracks, which had been spread across a kilometre wide track through the sand, changed into a tarmac road beginning right in the middle of the desert. Tiny trees, each one covered with a roof of palm leaves for protection against the sun's rays, cast meagre shadows on the boiling hot tarmac. In vain did we seek the Baghdad of our imagination from the Thousand and One Nights. Our thoughts were shattered by the sound of roaring engines as a giant bird of gleaming metal rose into the air just beside the roadway.

A modern airport, albeit of modest dimensions, is not the least that Baghdad has to offer: it has its own football team, modern petrol stations, Boy Scouts' organisations and a modern museum. Baghdad of the East is acquiring more and more Western features. You have to leave the modern main street and lose yourself in the narrow winding alleyways if you want to find the Baghdad of days gone by. Before the First World War the entire city consisted of a vast tangle of these little bazaar streets, and to get from one side of the city to the other meant a journey three times as long as the distance. Even the Turkish troops were obliged to take this roundabout route during the war, until the Turkish commander-in-chief in Iraq, Hallil Pasha, solved the traffic problem by building a dead-straight road parallel to the Tigris, which the British then named New Street. It is a strange contrast to the maze of dark branching alleys running through the rest of Baghdad.

Ctesiphon, the Parthian palace near Baghdad, photographed in 1888 by the archæologist Robert Koldewey. Both sides of the palace are in good condition.

Ctesiphon in a British aerial photograph of 1933, taken around the time when we visited the ruins. The right front of the palace had been undermined and washed away by the flooding of the Tigris (seen in the background).

Ctesiphon as it was when I visited it on a study trip in 1952. The back wall has partly broken away. Since then a fine park has been laid out around the royal palace of the Sassanids and Parthians.

Babylon at the time of Nebuchadnezzar II, about 600 BC (reconstruction). In the middle of the processional way is the Ishtar Gate through which Alexander the Great entered as victor. The full-sized Ishtar Gate now stands in the Pergamon Museum in Berlin.

However, the real centre of Baghdad today is still the Tigris to which the city owes its existence in the barren desert. On hot summer evenings, the river offers a pleasant coolness, and the coffee houses established along its banks are well-patronised. Boys and men smoke their hubble-bubbles in a dignified fashion, but not a single woman can be seen. Even now women must remain within the confines of the women's apartments at home.

Even so, sometimes in the late evening, black muffled figures hasten down to the river. They light little oil lamps which they consign nervously to the flow of the softly murmuring river. Slowly the little lights glide down the quiet stream, but the smallest wave can extinguish them. When one of the little flickering lights suddenly goes out, then the dark figure that set it afloat will sink to the ground wailing. By this sign Allah has informed her that she will never gain the love of the man in question. The other figures stand proudly gazing after their little love boats until the tiny lights disappear in the distance.

In winter, though, when heavy grey rainclouds hang above the city, the river rises higher and waves break over its banks. Then, when the snow begins to melt in the mountains of Asia Minor, the gurgling muddy waters pour out into the desert for many kilometres, turning it into a huge lake. But these winter floods last only a short while, for then spring comes. It seems wilder and more unruly than in Europe, but is, if anything, more idyllic. Green shoots spring up in the fields as soon as the waters go down. The desert, saturated with water, is adorned with flowers and herbs which transform the flat sandy country into a shimmering carpet in which the splendid blossoms form wonderful patterns, reminiscent of oriental weaving. The sun shines down with a pleasant warmth out of a cloudless sky, but its arc rises higher and higher and, after a few days the lush carpet of plants is burnt up by the sun's furnace and crumbles away into grey dust once more.

The heat, reaching as high as 57°C, becomes more and more unbearable. People retreat into the cellars of their homes, which afford some protection. Shafts connecting the cellars to the rooftops capture every movement of air and thus maintain a bearable temperature. The dust in the street seems to glow. Dogs and barefoot children leap in great strides when they are obliged to cross the open street between the shadows of the houses. The sun in Iraq is truly lethal, as the following case demonstrates.

A German soldier stationed in Baghdad during the First World War rested in the shade of a palm tree in order to avoid the worst of the heat. As he slept, the shadow of the tree moved round like the finger of a sundial and left him in the open. When he woke up two hours later, he felt slightly dizzy, but had just enough strength to drag himself into a cool bazaar alleyway where he died shortly afterwards.

Not until after sunset does the heat become bearable. Then the whole population of Baghdad migrates to the rooftops to partake of the evening meal. At night the beds of the inhabitants can be seen on all the roofs. Some are protected with mosquito nets and when a slight breeze wafts across the city they resemble small fantastical ships with swelling sails.

This murderous heat is nevertheless the authorities' best ally in the fight against those epidemics which are often transmitted by vermin. In the whole of Baghdad, you will not find a single bedbug or flea, since the ground here has become too hot for them. An emir from Baghdad was once on a study tour of Europe. He visited schools, hospitals, sports clubs and also a prison. This exalted gentleman from the East could not understand why it was a punishment to live in cells which seemed to his mind so comfortably furnished. They tried to explain it to him – loss of freedom, monotonous food, and above all, bedbugs. The potentate had never before heard of bedbugs. He demanded a thorough explanation of the creature's life-cycle and habits and then decided that, in order to punish his own prisoners more harshly, he would transplant a few hundred of these pests into the prisons of Baghdad. He returned home full of what he had learnt and carrying two specimen jars of bedbugs. But alas, his attempts at prison reform were to end in disappointment, for within a week not one of the European bedbugs was left alive. They were no match for the terrible climate.

I wandered through Baghdad's narrow alleyways. With great effort I had succeeded in eluding my hotel manager who had talked me into having not only a bath but also a European five-course dinner. It also cost me no small effort to get rid of a business-minded old Arab. This 'proud son of the desert' first wanted to show me wonderful 'Arab dancing girls' – for a suitable baksheesh, of course – but in the end he would have been quite happy just to sell me genuine Arab jewellery 'made in Germany.'

I left behind modern New Street with its hotels and automobiles and white-clad policemen who gave you very hard looks if you crossed the street without due care. I walked between high mud walls, seeing only the occasional little doorway. A foreigner could walk around Baghdad all day and see nothing but these windowless walls, for Arab life goes on well away from prying eyes, but also well away from the sun's rays, in the interior of the house. In this maze of lifeless grey walls the bazaar is the only pleasant variation: covered arched throughways, full of the manifold life of the East. The further I penetrated into the bazaar, the less real and more magical became the scene. Arabs swathed in their white robes slipped past me on soft soles, shopkeepers stared at me in amazement. One who was leafing through the Koran, shook his fist at me threateningly. What right had I, an infidel, to come here disturbing their peace out of mere curiosity?

The skylights letting in the harsh sun became less frequent, and the corridors of the bazaar were shadowy and dark. Only the white robes and sharp features of the Arabs pierced the murky gloom.

In one corner huddled a blind old man, reciting the thousand-year-old folk tales of Arabia to a respectful audience. Sometimes he would feel about with satisfaction in his begging bowl which was slowly filling up with copper coins. Here in the bazaar, Baghdad has remained as it was centuries ago, and here we can still find the Baghdad of *One Thousand and One Nights*.

After the first few days of excitement and disappointment, we remembered what we were meant to be doing. Only three thousand nine hundred kilometres had been covered so far, and ahead of us lay another ten thousand or so kilometres of difficulty and uncertainty before our far-off destination: India.

Stopping in a large city always entails much organisational work. Added to which, one is desperately eager to get mail. After hearing nothing about home for weeks at a time, getting all those letters at the consulate is like Christmas. Letters are opened with joy and apprehension at the same time. It was no joke dealing with

The tomb of Zobeida, favourite wife of Haroun al Rashid, in Baghdad. After the famous caliph was poisoned near Meshed in Eastern Persia, it was the clever Zobeida who took over the government, a unique event in the Orient, where women in general had no say. But, in Islam, too, it's the exception that proves the rule. This splendid tomb for a woman is likewise a unique exception.

our sponsors. They were calculating businessmen who had laid out a stack of good Alpendollars so that we two lads could go off and see the world. I once received a letter which read as follows:

*"On the basis of the travel schedule presented by you to the management committee, you should have been in $Z$ two weeks ago. Unfortunately we see from your last telegram that you are only in $X$, and that in consequence of your change of route you will not pass through $Y$ at all. Please provide an explanation."*

Wham! Letters like this were a pain. My friends know that, as well as the Puch Works – which always generous and sympathetic – there were many, many other companies, institutions and scientific bodies who had contributed their mite towards the costs of the journey. The less this was, the more important it seemed to be to the donors.

When it came to replying to an annoying letter from home, I gladly took refuge behind the Austrian Consulate. A word from here was worth more than a hundred from me, and because of their local knowledge they were in a much better position to give an effective explanation and to point out that the view of Asia from behind a desk in Europe was very different from the reality on the ground.

I was jolly glad to find that all our local representatives knew we were coming.

| Baghdad: a Bedouin from the desert has come into town to dictate a letter to a scribe.

The Federal Chancellery (Foreign Affairs) had given us a special recommendation and requested the Austrian embassies, legations and consulates in Asia to give us introductions to local officials. The reasons for our enterprise were expressed in a document from the Federal Chancellery in the following terms:

*"The aim of the trip is to provide proof that an extended journey can be made through difficult terrain even with a light motorcycle, and also to make the Puch cycle known abroad. Max Reisch, who will be unarmed, will be carrying photographic and ciné cameras, a tent and other items of equipment."*

We were indeed unarmed and I have always considered this the best life-insurance. What use would a revolver be anyway? It is part of the Asian mentality that they will only attack a white person when they are certain of military superiority, so what good would we do with one or two revolvers against a band of twenty men?

So we were unarmed and we faced up to many a tricky encounter with a beaming boyish smile and strict self-control, achieving more this way than with a weapon in our hand.

In Baghdad we had much work to do regarding immigration formalities for Persia, and we also gave the motorcycle a thorough check. We had to do it all ourselves, of course, because I wouldn't have let anyone else touch our faithful Puch, and anyway, Asian mechanics in those days hadn't a clue about motorcycles. For some years a motorcycle had only rarity value on that continent.

In Baghdad I at last discovered the fault that had been driving me mad all across

The Golden Mosque of Kazimayn near Baghdad: a Persian Shi'ite shrine within the Sunni Arabic world. Islam, too, has its internal problems.

the Syrian desert and lay over us like a heavy shadow. It must have been the weirdest thing to go wrong with a motorcycle that any rider has ever experienced. The bike ran absolutely faultlessly the whole way through the desert, only sometimes when there was good weather and a smooth surface, I would open up a bit and go over 50kph. Then something dreadful would happen – there would be a hard knock, the whole machine would shudder and rattle about and simultaneously lose speed. Often it was so bad that I thought the whole engine would fly apart. Since this disturbing phenomenon only manifested itself at higher speeds, i.e. when I tried to use third gear, I decided quite reasonably that there must be a fault with the gears. A nut or split-pin must have come undone and was wreaking havoc in the gearbox. My forehead was constantly breaking out in sweat from fear, and in the end I simply did not dare use third gear any more. More than once I came near to opening the gearbox so that I could get to the bottom of the mystery, but I was always held back by the lead seals which had been attached to all the essential components. To get back to Vienna with the seals intact was a prime aim.

For the first time an expedition was going to provide real proof of performance. The untouched lead seals were a guarantee that no important component had been replaced.

(True to their word, even amid all the excitement of our welcome home in Vienna, stern-faced officials arrived and subjected the seals to close examination – all were still there and all were unbroken. I was justly proud of this, because I know the true stories behind plenty of other expeditions and I know that not everything is always as wonderful as the reports would have you believe. The engineers from Puch came from Graz to Vienna to welcome us and we shook hands over and over again in mutual congratulation. We were all extremely happy.)

I had got as far as picking up a pair of pliers, ready to prise the seals apart and then dismantle the gearbox. I feared that the awful nerve-racking judder would start happening in first and second gear as well, and then it would be 'curtains.' All the same, I couldn't quite pluck up courage to undo the seals. Perhaps a miracle would happen after all. So we crawled all the way to Baghdad in the two lower gears. There was no miracle, but we did find the solution to the mystery. This solution was ludicrously simple and lay in a completely different area from the one I'd suspected. I'm almost ashamed to have to tell the story. As I was giving the machine a thorough check and clean-up in the yard of the Tigris Palace Hotel, I noticed that the back mudguard was bent and was clearing the back tyre by only a few millimetres. It must have happened as we were crossing an area of scree and had several collisions with large stones. At any normal speed it did no harm, as the back wheel could still move freely. However, when the tyre expanded in the heat and when its circumference was further enlarged at higher speeds in third gear by centrifugal force, then the blocks of the tyre tread caught intermittently on the bent end of the mudguard.

In addition to this, the wheel rim was no longer running quite true because of broken spokes. The fortuitous combined effect of all these factors meant that the tyre blocks sometimes got hooked up on the bent mudguard so badly that it led to shuddering and knocking in the entire machine! To think how I had agonised about it the whole way through the desert! And now all I needed was a strong pair of pliers to bend back the mudguard, and the 'major defect' was sorted!

I could thank the seals for that, for without them I should certainly have taken the gearbox apart without any certainty of being able to reassemble it, although I'm not usually put off by mechanical jobs.

In spite of our worries – in fact, only one worry, which was, 'Will we get to India?' – we enjoyed Baghdad and all it had to offer. Almost every evening we would sail upstream on the motor launch belonging to the German Embassy and bathe in the Tigris, in company with the German Ambassador and the archaeologist Professor Jordan.

# 6
# CAUTION IN KARBALA

Since we had heard so much about the city of Karbala, we made a detour to see it. Together with Benares and Mecca, Karbala can claim to rank among the holiest of cities which millions of the faithful yearn to visit. Situated on the northern edge of the Arabian desert, barely a hundred kilometres from Baghdad, the city with its low mud houses offers nothing exceptional to the eye, but its significance for the Moslem world is great, for it holds the tomb of Hussein, second son of the Caliph Ali. After the murder of Ali in the 7th century, Hussein attempted to become his father's successor and seize the Caliphate. At the battle of Karbala, he and his loyal followers were slain by the Umayyads, since when the place of Hussein's martyrdom has become the principal shrine of the Shi'ites, the followers of Ali. For these people a pilgrimage to the mosque where Hussein lies buried is thus more important and more commendable than a journey to Mecca.

The population of Karbala, which numbers about forty thousand, is increasing faster than that of any other city in Iraq. During the main pilgrimage season there are sometimes as many as two hundred thousand pilgrims in the city, travelling from India, the Caucasus and Central Asia. The inhabitants of Karbala earn their living largely by providing bed and board for the visitors.

Entry to the Mosque of the Tomb is strictly forbidden to Europeans, or more precisely, to non-Moslems. Until now, only Lawrence of Arabia is said to have gained entry to the shrine. Having expert knowledge of the East and of the Arabic language, he disguised himself as an Arab, mixed with the crowd and got into the mosque unrecognised. To understand the danger of this undertaking, one must be aware of the fanaticism of Moslems, who would rather die an agonising death than see their shrines desecrated by an infidel. Even today in the narrow alleyways of Karbala one may not escape a stoning by religious fanatics who see fewer than a dozen Europeans in the course of a year.

We reached Karbala in the early evening. Above the forest of palm trees which surrounds the city for a kilometre on all sides, tower the golden domes of the mosques, making a picture of improbable beauty in the setting sun. Whereas in Baghdad with its dust, dirt and traffic, any trace of the Thousand and One Nights is hard to find, here it comes alive quite naturally.

We still had one difficulty ahead – finding somewhere to spend the night, for there was not a single inn in Karbala which would give shelter to the infidel. No European was allowed to spend the night within the holy city. But we had a letter of introduction to the mayor, given to us by a Polish doctor from Baghdad who had enormous influence throughout Arabia, and this now proved invaluable. We were immediately welcomed into the mayor's house, although he was out at the time. But just as we were about to go out for a walk around the town, the servant explained to us that we were not allowed to leave the house alone. It would be too dangerous if we were seen by fanatics walking at this hour in the twilit streets. At my insistence we were at last permitted to go a little way through the city, but two soldiers followed us to give protection and keep an eye on us. They made scrupulous efforts to keep us away from the mosque.

With the heat of the day over, the streets were now very busy. The men sat outside their houses in the street and smoked long hubble-bubbles. Fruit and water sellers cried their wares in loud voices. By the looks they gave us, people seemed somewhat taken aback but not exactly unfriendly. Only the mullahs – Moslem clerics recognisable by their turbans – regarded us with hostility. We drank a small glass of lemonade at a little bar. As we paid, the proprietor meticulously avoided touching my hand. Then he took the glasses away into the back room and the next thing we heard was a sound of breaking glass. The man had smashed the glasses we had just drunk from because they had become unclean through contact with Christians and therefore unusable. Both before this and later I knew Moslems and Hindus to throw away the dishes from which we had eaten, but the act of hospitality rates so highly in the East that it may present the host with difficulties impossible for Europeans to comprehend.

When we returned to the house, we found the master was already there, a tall dignified old man, who shook us warmly by the hand. An interpreter translated his Arabic greeting into English for us. He said he was very happy that we had done him the honour of a visit and that we should regard his house as our own. I replied in the flowery oriental manner that it had for many years been our great and insatiable desire to see Karbala and that we were delighted by the beauty of the city and the kindness of its inhabitants.

The evening meal was served out on the flat roof of the house. We took rice and mutton with our fingers from a common dish about the size of a small washbasin. A dessert of sweet dates followed – our hands were sticky to the wrists with this opulent meal. Soon our host took his leave and withdrew to the company of his wife and children, whose faces we never saw during the whole of our stay in his house. I later learned it was a mark of great honour that the mayor had eaten with us out of one dish.

Meanwhile darkness had fallen and only the minarets of the mosque, illuminated by a thousand lights, shone out to us across the sleeping city. There was a distant sound of prayers from some of the faithful and above it all rose the vault of the cloudless southern sky, full of stars.

The next morning we were guided through the city by a young Arab who spoke fluent English. We were allowed to go quite near the mosque and even to peer though the door at the inside. I asked our guide what would happen if we entered. He just smiled and said "You certainly would not get out alive." He pointed at the

Persian Kurdistan: the village Aga (Lord) with his wives. Three are carrying water, the fourth is at home cooking. The weight of one of these goatskin waterbags when full is around 30 to 35kg.

A girl from Karind, an exclusively Kurdish settlement in the Persian Zagros Mountains. The Kurds are Moslems, but their women go unveiled. This girl is still unmarried and wears her dowry openly in the form of chains of silver and gold coins.

On the border between Iraq and Persia near Kanikin. It was so hot that we had to cover the machine, otherwise we would have burned our hands on the controls.

people standing around who were giving us dark looks. I tried taking a few steps nearer to the doorway, but immediately there were Arabs in my way, reaching in a menacing way for their daggers. This was proof enough for me and I gladly gave up any further attempts.

There were not many pilgrims in Karbala at this time, but in Muharram, the Shi'ite holy month, the city is overflowing with the faithful making their pilgrimage to the holy tombs (as well as Hussein, his brother Hassan is also buried here). Indians, Persians and Arabs often come thousands of kilometres on foot to satisfy their yearning for this city. It is moreover the dearest wish of every believer to be buried here, near to Hussein. When a man feels his death approaching, he will travel to Karbala in order to die here. There are also many who, unable to reach the city before they die, make provision for their bodies to be carried to Karbala.

Karbala's bazaar may not be as magnificent as the one in Istanbul, but it is quite unspoilt, since it is only rarely that a European wanders into this part of the true Orient. The little alleys of the bazaar are roofed over as protection against the burning heat and lie in cool semi-darkness. A special guild of craftsmen is responsible for producing souvenirs for the pilgrims. High prices are paid for cotton cloths that have been washed in the water of the Euphrates and laid out for a night on Hussein's tomb. They also manufacture amulets from Karbala's soil to give protection against illness, little cubes of clay with inscriptions from the Koran, giving them a double value. Alongside these cubes in the bazaar may be seen strange pointed implements which are used by the faithful during the great festivals of atonement to pierce themselves in the breast. The shop owners sit cross-legged among their wares, staring ahead with indifference, some piously reading aloud from the Koran. In a little side street we saw an old man with a white beard who had spread out his prayer mat and was bowing towards Mecca in the rhythm of Moslem prayer.

As soon as the month of Muharram arrives, the quiet tranquil life of the city is transformed into an orgy of blood. This is the time when the death of Hussein is celebrated as the greatest festival of atonement in the Shiah. The religious pageant depicting the murder of Hussein is then performed in nearly every town and village of Shi'ite Islam, but nowhere is it presented on such a scale and with such fanatical cruelty as in Karbala itself, the place where he was murdered.

The evening before the festival, all doorways are decked with banners which are black as a sign of mourning. The stage is set up in the market place of Karbala. People squat in their thousands around the edge of the square and on the roofs of the adjoining houses. The women hidden under their heavy black robes resemble a flock of black crows. The festival is opened by flagellants with chains. They wear dark clothes but with the back and the breast left bare, and carry a scourge in their right hand. The scourge is made up of a short wooden handle with ten or twenty iron chains hanging from it. They stride forward to the sound of drums, constantly beating themselves on the back with the chains, at every stroke calling out the name of Hussein. The sun burns down pitilessly on their tortured backs covered with bloody weals. Next come the breast beaters, old men who are mostly servants of the mosque, all of whom are said to be direct descendants of the Prophet. As a sign of mourning they wear dark-coloured turbans and strike their breasts with bare fists.

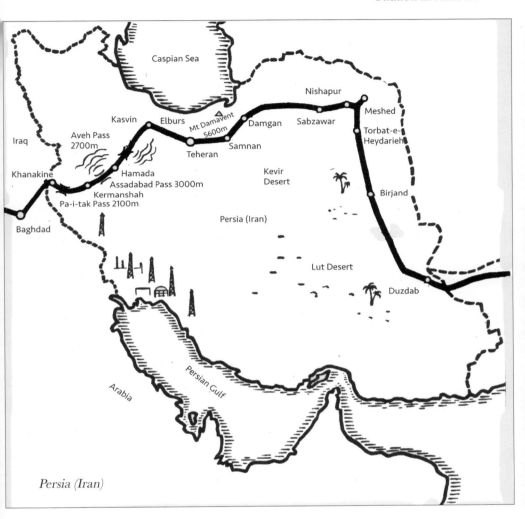

Persia (Iran)

*VISIT VELOCE ON THE WEB – WWW.VELOCE.CO.UK*
*All current books • New book news • Special offers • Gift vouchers • Forum*

77

# 7
# THE FIRST GREAT CRISIS

While in Baghdad we had heard of another motorcyclist somewhere ahead of us who was also intending to get to India. This made me a bit uneasy, because who can honestly say, hand on heart, that competition is welcome? I would not have been too pleased by arriving in India in second place.

I was naturally all agog to find out more. Who was it? What country were they from? What machine were they riding?

At the border between Iraq and Persia, where we were held up for a whole day, I had plenty of opportunity to make inquiries. From the local records I was able to make out that the man was Walter Tonn from Hannover, riding a 750cc Indian-Mabeco with a sidecar. He had a massive start on us, having crossed the border five weeks previously. Would I ever succeed in catching up with Walter Tonn? It seemed unlikely. Our light motorcycle compared very unfavourably with his heavier machine.

I confess that this business irked me very much, but in the meantime things turned out very differently, and I am sorry that I grudged Walter Tonn his five weeks advantage. We did indeed catch up with him, and soon. We found him, and yet we didn't. In Kermanshah we stood by his grave – he had died here of sandfly fever and typhus about two weeks before.

Dear God, that really shook us – that poor little grave on the edge of the Moslem cemetery, still so fresh and yet already abandoned and forgotten.

The Indian-Mabeco machine stood on flat tyres in one corner of the yard of the caravanserai, already half cannibalised. Its master was dead and so was the machine.

Yet again, the land route to India had shown no mercy. Quite apart from the victims claimed every year by the Kavir and Lut deserts, this is where one of the world's great military disasters took place. During his return from India, Alexander the Great lost ten thousand men through exhaustion and lack of water in the Persian desert. Consequently, this caravan route has been known throughout the ages as the Road of the Ten Thousand.

The fate of Walter Tonn affected us very deeply. I made no mention of this tragic occurrence in the reports for newspapers which I was writing throughout the journey. It would only have made our parents and friends more anxious than they already were. Today, I am able to write about it and to acknowledge that the lonely grave in Kermanshah marked a great crisis in our trip. Although we had not known Walter Tonn personally, we nevertheless felt a close bond with him, and we lost all enthusiasm for the journey, even though we had been pretty annoyed when we first heard of a rival ahead of us.

The crisis affected us in various ways. We asked ourselves why we were subjecting ourselves to all this physical strain instead of staying comfortably at home. Instead of risking our lives here under the burning sun in Persia, we could have been lying on a beach by a lake in our own country, with a nice girl. That would have been vastly preferable!

Thoughts like this are dangerous. Fortunately, we recognised this in time and took counter measures to beat the crisis. This usually took the form of swearing at each other very violently by mutual agreement. We gave each other a thorough psychological shake-up: there was to be no weakening. Life must go on. Getting to our grand destination was worth our best efforts. Gradually, the fairytale quest cast its spell over us once more.

Now we went north again, not in a straight line, but in a general direction. After a few more hours crossing the flat ground of the desert, we left the Arab world, and had to convert our hard-won knowledge of Iraqi currency – fils, annas, rupees – into Persian krans and tomans. In Iraq we had spent almost no money, apart from in Baghdad. Mr Roggers took responsibility for our main expense, ie petrol and oil, and we had gone several hundred kilometres on Iraqi territory before we effected our first purchases in Baghdad. The friendly Bedouin and peasants along the Euphrates could never be prevailed upon to take anything from us, and they shared with us anything they had: bread, dates, cucumbers, sometimes black coffee.

Another set of border formalities (just for the record, these took nine hours), and we were in Persia. However, this is no longer Persia, it is Iran – a new name promising nationalism and reform, which is fulfilled in part anyway.

A new world begins at the border: different people, a different language, a different landscape. No more proud Arabs, but men who have broken with their own proud, albeit crumbling past, and are as yet uncertain of the place they will occupy in the new world that Reza Shah is planning for them. No more the hard guttural tones of Arabic, but the smoother, polished Persian language. No more the flat, monotonous, and yet ever-delightful plain of Mesopotamia, but a hilly country, at first just low bare hills, not much different from the plain with a few slopes and dips.

Soon, though, these became proper great mountains with deep hollow valleys. It was a surprise every time we found a road leading out of one of these gigantic mousetraps. The road went uphill and downhill, but mostly up, and soon the cool, almost cold air of the Iranian highlands was blowing around us.

Only a few kilometres beyond Kermanshah is the mountain of Bisutun. In antiquity, this was the site of the decisive battle between Darius and the unfortunate Fravartish, who was defeated and taken prisoner. At the foot of the near-vertical eastern face of the mountain rises a great spring of clear water, which is of course extremely important to this arid country. Here was the residence of the Sassanid rulers from Ardashir I to Khossrou II. At the base of a cliff surrounded by a crystal clear lake are two caves decorated with rock carvings, called Tak-i-Bustan.

Persian baker's shop. The bread is thin and about the size of a towel. Outside the bakery the flatbreads hang on poles ready for sale. The bread tastes excellent when fresh.

Some of these rock carvings were done in the 6th century and some only a few decades ago, and they show various symbolic or glorified scenes from the lives of the rulers.

I owe this archaeological information to the editor of an art magazine. After my return, I sent him the photographs I had taken of the carvings and he did an article on them, full of facts and erudition. It was a pity that we did not have him with us when we were lying in the shade resting at Tak-i-Bustan.

The Pa-i-tak pass was behind us but we still had the Assadabad pass to negotiate. We found this Assadabad Pass very demanding. It is 3000 metres high, and we had just come from Baghdad which is only 200 metres above sea level. Such differences in altitude are quite unknown in Europe. The air was thin, the track was steep and stony, and with our crazily overloaded machine I could have done with some sort of crank to pedal us up. At the top of the pass we were miserably cold in our tropical tent. The snow-covered sides of the Persian mountains, over 5000 metres high, seemed near enough to touch. This was indeed a contrast – a few days ago we had been in the burning heat of Baghdad, and now this icy mountain environment! Then it was down again into a bare, sun-scorched valley and up once more to the Aveh Pass at an altitude of 2600 metres. After that we were through the mountainous fringes of Persia and were now in the bowl of the central Persian desert.

On our last lap to Teheran, it seemed that fate overtook us. We both had badly grazed legs. This is unavoidable on a motorcycle, especially if you are riding barelegged because of the heat. Then of course there is always dust and dirt so that wounds heal badly and frequently go septic. We had got used to this and attached no great importance to any of it, but we got worried about one of Herbert's wounds: the flesh around it was a nasty blue-black colour. In Hamadan we considered resting up for a bit, but then decided to keep going to Teheran. Somewhere along the road we came across some hot springs (called Ab-e-Garm, 'hot water') and although I was against it, Herbert would not be dissuaded from taking a good long bath. The hot water had some sort of deleterious effect on his system, so that by evening he had a fever and his leg was so painful that he could no longer sit on the bike. We spent a sleepless night in our little tent which we put up by the roadside. The night was full of stars, and around us rose the silhouettes of the mountains, dark and forbidding like our own dismal thoughts. It was only a few days back that I had seen Walter Tonn's motorcycle. I am not usually prone to pessimism, but with the image of the German grave in Kermanshah and Herbert delirious beside me ... There are moments when one thinks, to hell with such a trip, and wishes one had never had such a ridiculous idea as going to India by motorcycle.

For me, that was probably the longest and most terrible night of the whole journey. Herbert knew very little about it, and, when morning came, he said, "I think we ought to stop now. It's getting dark."

His leg was heavily swollen, and he couldn't move. I didn't know what to do. Go back to Hamadan? Or on to Kasvin? Get help? But from whom? There were no doctors in those towns. No, better wait here. There must be a vehicle along some time going in the direction of Teheran. Wait, then. I gave Herbert 'Ovaltine' dissolved in water.

At last in the distance I heard the sound of an engine, coming from the direction of Hamadan. Would the driver be friendly? I hadn't had much experience of Persian lorry drivers up till now. They all looked very wild and did not inspire confidence.

Now the vehicle came round the bend. It was a high, heavily loaded lorry. I stood in the middle of the road and waved madly as I'd never waved in my life before. The lorry never slackened its speed but bore down upon me as if I wasn't there.

The Lallesar, the main street of Teheran, in 1933. Teheran was then a large village with about 250,000 inhabitants. Today, it has 5 million.

At the last moment I jumped aside. But now the vehicle was stopping. It had just driven on a few metres to a flat place. The driver came back, looking exactly as I had imagined, dissolute and angry.

He spoke a few words of French and I pointed to Herbert. I scraped together my entire knowledge of French and Persian in order to persuade the driver to take Herbert with him. I was so agitated that I forgot this time to work in the proverb about Isfahan, even though it had always had a soothing effect, even on the most infuriated policeman.

I was no more than half way through my appeal to the philanthropy of Persian lorry drivers in general, and the good heart of this gentleman in particular, when the driver picked up Herbert in his arms like a baby and carried him to the lorry, saying over and over, "Doctor ... Teheran ... quickly!" He made a soft bed out of blankets and furs in between the bags and boxes, and tied Herbert on to it with ropes for greater safety.

Then began the wildest ride of my life. Without a pillion passenger, the machine leapt around on the rough road like a mad thing, and the lorry in front drove as if the Devil himself were after it. Sometimes it was nothing but a cloud of dust way ahead on the horizon, and going through the mountains I lost it from sight entirely. In Kasvin we made a long halt, and as there was a heavy sandstorm coming up, decided to spend the night there.

The Persian driver was a splendid chap. He found shelter for Herbert at an inn and forced him to swallow large doses of raki, saying, "Medicine! Medicine!." He was evidently afraid of infection, as he was not averse to this medicine himself. Soon I was likewise so far gone that I was able to inform him in faltering tones that Isfahan was half the world, at which he appeared as happy and highly honoured as if he had built the said city all by himself.

By the middle of the following day we reached Teheran and drove straight to a hospital. The doctors looked very grave when they saw Herbert. They talked about amputating the leg, saying that it was poisoned to such an extent that a radical operation was the only way to save his life. I pleaded with the doctors to wait another day and give Herbert any sort of medicine that might help, in the hopes that the

Stopping for a rest in the Persian highlands. Between Baghdad and Teheran we had to get over three passes on steep, stony tracks. The Assadabad Pass, 3000 metres high, put quite a strain on the engine because of the thin air.

poisoning might subside. The doctors agreed to wait one more day, in the course of which the swelling went down so much that there was no more talk of amputation, and a week later, Herbert was up and about in perfect health.

As for the lorry driver whom Herbert probably had to thank for saving his leg, if not his life, he had disappeared without trace after delivering us to the hospital. We owed him not just for the leg, but also for a copious supper and a huge quantity of raki, all of which he had provided for us in Kasvin. In Teheran, he had lifted Herbert down from the lorry and then just driven off, as if picking up sick motorcyclists from the roadside and transporting them to Teheran was all in a day's work.

I did however know the number of his lorry, and with the help of a German friend and the police, we soon succeeded in finding him. He looked very surprised and somewhat apprehensive when we turned up at his house in the company of a policeman who had been acting as our driver. Very likely he was not on especially good terms with the Teheran police, for he looked at our policeman as if all he could expect was unpleasantness. Not until he understood that we were only seeking him out in order to thank him did he grin broadly and say laughing, "Isfahan is half the world – we friends!" He could not be persuaded to accept money from us, and so we invited him to an impressive banquet in the best restaurant in Teheran.

We must have caused no less of a sensation with the international clientele, since we did not fit into any category of customer normally to be found in this expensive establishment. We didn't look like diplomats or crooks or spies, but we had a very jolly evening.

*VISIT VELOCE ON THE WEB – WWW.VELOCE.CO.UK*
*All current books • New book news • Special offers • Gift vouchers • Forum*

84

# THE PARIS OF THE EAST

We had not just one but many jolly evenings in Teheran. Many cities famously claim to be the Paris of the Orient but as far as I can judge, this title best fits Teheran. Outwardly it does not much resemble the metropolis on the River Seine. The main streets are straight and modern, and like most modern streets in Asian cities, somewhat lacking in taste. Alongside these modern streets lies a warren of narrow alleyways: dirty, delightful, and truly Asian. At the time of our journey Persia was intent on becoming 'western' as quickly as possible, and was ashamed of these little streets – similarly of camel caravans. We heard of a German journalist who was deported from Persia because his paper had published an illustrated article by him showing the modern post office building in Teheran with a camel caravan in the foreground. These innocent camels nearly caused a diplomatic incident, being seen by the Persians as a mockery of their country's progress.

But I am getting away from explaining why Teheran is a Paris of the east. I believe it has something to do with that peculiar feminine headdress called the chador. This is half way between a hat and a veil, a sort of compromise between western progress which demands that women's faces be open and unveiled, and the Asian tradition which prefers to veil women. It is a very charming compromise. Beneath the nose a sort of black curtain hangs across the face, providing a veil for the mouth and chin, but leaving the eyes free. And what eyes! They are large and black and fiery. As a headcovering, ladies in Teheran also wear a black thing that could be described as a hat. This is the upper part of the chador which has a broad edge like a brim sticking out over the forehead, rather like the peak of a sports cap but much bigger. A lady dressed in this way only has to bow her head a little for the brim to cover the open part of her face, making her look as if she is completely veiled. But unlike a veil that is all-enveloping and uncompromising, it can in fact be relaxed to a certain degree by raising or lowering the head – according to personal choice, so to speak. It is extraordinary what effects are achieved by the ladies of Teheran with this simple modern device. You see a black ghostly figure coming towards you, so black and impersonal that the male imagination is left completely cold, even though you would normally not let slip such a promising opportunity. Any firm basis or starting point on which to build the flimsiest of fantasies is completely lacking. This deficiency is soon remedied by the chador and a skilful movement of the wearer's head. Suddenly there

In the foreground are three Persian women with the usual chador of those days. The peak jutting forward over the eyes makes it possible to reveal or conceal the face by a slight raising or lowering of the head. This was often quite a flirtatious little game. In the background are two Russian women, émigrées from the Soviet Union.

In the Persian capital Teheran, cars were already familiar, but no one had yet seen a motorcycle. A highly suspicious vehicle! We had to go and demonstrate it in the courtyard of a police barracks. I rode a few artistic figures-of-eight and was then presented with this splendid document – the first Persian motorcycle licence.

are two big dark eyes looking at you, and what a look they give! The protection of the chador makes many inhibitions unnecessary, since the next moment they can slip back again behind its anonymity. Starting from a pair of eyes like that, the imagination can run riot! So on the one hand, the chador provokes masculine thoughts, leading to desire and to action, and on the other hand it permits the ladies at any given moment – that is, at the moment they think desirable – to behave in as open and inviting a manner as if they were not ladies at all. It also enables them, in the fraction of a second that it takes to bow the head, to change back into an impersonal black figure. It is amazing what an exhilarating effect these two options produce in everyday life. I am not making some idle or superficial comment when I say that Teheran deserves to be called the Paris of the East: I know what I'm talking about.

We consequently spent quite a long time in Teheran, much longer than we had originally intended, and longer than the directors of Steyr-Daimler-Puch found acceptable. They wrote us reminders full of suspicious questions and fatherly admonition. Of course, it would have been quite impossible to explain to the worthy company directors how monotonous was a motorcycle ride through the desert and how charming was an evening stroll in Teheran, with all the psychological conclusions that would be drawn, and so I wrote back that Herbert was not yet quite well enough after his blood-poisoning to allow us to think about going on with the journey. Of course, since Herbert wrote at the same time to inform his worried father that he was completely recovered, and his father was in close contact with the board of directors, this gave rise to a certain degree of misunderstanding which could only be resolved by a definite farewell to the Persian capital. Before this, however, I had been obliged to wage a small war with the Persian customs office.

Our new Semperit tyres were waiting for us. They had made the long journey all the way across Russia to Persia and I was overjoyed to find them at last in the Persian customs shed. We needed them – could we have them, please?

"No," said the Persian chief of customs. Indeed they were here, and he also knew that I was the only person in all Persia who could use them, since there were no other motorcycles in the country, but, unfortunately, he was unable to give me the tyres. "Why not?" "Because there was no Persian import licence."

I could have throttled the man. He was a sadist. He even had the tyres brought to his office and placed next to his desk. He showed them to me, but did not hand them over. I came to a decision not to throttle him but to take his picture. I photographed him in the office, with the tyres, without the tyres, outside the customs shed, alone, then with his employees around him. Then I photographed his house, him outside his house, him under the pomegranate tree in his garden, him with his children, then his children, then each child individually.

I spent all night developing and printing in a Persian photographer's darkroom, handed him the pictures and received the tyres. The Europeans in Teheran said I had brought off a great diplomatic coup. This deserved a celebration, in a Persian bar no less. Of course, we donned the best clothes we had, our casually elegant plus-four suits. We danced enthusiastically with Persian girls and Russian girls. We were a sensational success, less on our own account than because of our plus-fours.

The next day a Persian came asking for us at the hotel. He was a journalist on the Shafar Sorgh newspaper. We gave him a full account of our trip and our objectives.

'Tower of silence' near Teheran. To the Parsees, followers of the religion of Zoroaster, fire, water and earth are sacred. For this reason they lay out their dead on towers like these and leave them to the vultures.

Shortly afterwards there arrived another man, a tailor by trade, saying that he had received orders for trousers such as we had been wearing in the bar yesterday. He begged to be allowed to see these trousers. We obliged. The day after, the reporter from the Shafar Sorgh returned bringing us his newspaper. There was nothing in it about our travels or what we were hoping to achieve, but only a very precise description of our trouserings. When the owner of the bar had a new sign with 'Knickerbocker Bar' put up over his establishment, we had had enough and made a hasty departure.

We left Teheran on 24th September 1933. Herbert had completely recovered from his blood-poisoning, and the machine was equipped with a new rear tyre. It was not really necessary, as the old tyre was still in perfect condition. We changed it nevertheless, although this was purely a precautionary measure, and rather an excessive one. When it came down to it, had I taken all that trouble with the Persian customs chief just to leave the tyres behind in Teheran? That would have been a terrible shame after all the effort with the forty-seven photographs that it had cost me to get them.

I never cease to marvel at these Semperit tyres. It must not be forgotten that our 'pantechnicon' was being carried on the pneumatic tyres of a light motorcycle. We were really a couple of irresponsible idiots, running heavily overloaded tyres on Asian roads, but these were pedigree tyres! The inner tube on the back wheel was constantly getting holes because of all the nails and we worked hard patching it, but the outer tyre suffered no damage at all.

It seemed very odd that we did not get a single puncture on the front wheel, considering we went thirteen thousand kilometres through Asia. Whenever Herbert felt homesick, I used to advise him to take a lungful of Viennese air out of the front tube! He actually did this on one occasion, in the Baluchistan desert when we were finding the salt dust and the heat so oppressive. "That's better!" he said. I fetched the pump in order to refill the tube, and as I looked up I saw Herbert staring happily into the distance, under the calming influence of home. "You try it!" he said, and so I took a lungful of Viennese air too and all the hardship of our journey suddenly became easier to bear.

The second of the tyres we had received from the Teheran customs was strapped on to our tent bag. The spares that one takes on a trip like this are usually not needed. They are there for reassurance. This was what happened with our third tyre – we brought it all the way home unused.

During our stay in Teheran the engine had been de-coked and had got its old powerful sound back. We had altogether 40 litres of petrol on board in the main tank, the two supplementary tanks and in a can behind Herbert's seat. On normal roads this is enough for about twelve hundred kilometres but here it would only take us seven to eight hundred kilometres. That was sufficient in Persia, because in the oases we got petrol from the Anglo-Iranian Oil Company and oil in sealed Shell cans.

We were in a good mood – anyway, we had been on the road for two months now and had covered half the distance to India. Could anything else go wrong? No, touch wood ...

The Austrian Consul accompanied us in his car to the eastern gate of Teheran. We watched dumbfounded as he produced from his car, as if by magic, a small bottle of Zierfandler (Austrian white wine) ... and so it was Prost! and a safe journey!

The royal mosque of Isfahan. 'Isfahan nesfi jihan aest'– 'Isfahan is half the world.' This proverb, known throughout Persia, implies that the sights of the old imperial city are worth as much as the rest of the world put together. If something wasn't going right, we often gained favour and support from the Persians by paying this compliment.

# 9
# DESERT FEVER AND A MISSIONARY

So how long was the next leg of the journey? About two thousand kilometres, our destination being Duzdab in southern Persia. After that would come another destination, and then another until at last, sometime, we would reach our final one. After that we would be home again, and after the first thrill of joy we would be smitten with wanderlust. We would feel suffocated by the tall buildings and crowds of people. We would have to go back to school and be ignorant and useless at college stuff, having sweated away the little we did know in the Persian desert, and the girls in our class would say, "Yes, he's quite nice, I suppose, and he did go to India, but he's terribly thick. It's no use copying his essays!"

This was all very sad, and often seemed to hang over us like a nightmare: to think that our great quest should have such a prosaic sequel. Back to school – we couldn't imagine it, and yet I remember clearly that this thought oppressed us quite frequently throughout the journey. Somehow, after it was all over, I still managed to pass all the exams. I still don't know to this day how on earth I did it, but I did somehow.

But at this stage we were only in Teheran, with many delightful experiences still to come. Soon we would fall under the spell of the mysterious desert of Dasht-i-Kavir and the treacherous desert of Lut. I was so looking forward to it!

The Leica was now working again, too. I forgot to tell you about that: I hope Herr Leitz in Wetzlar will permit it, and forgive me. He showed me round his factory and, as we were saying goodbye, he pressed into my hands the latest Leica model. This was most generous, and I take off my hat to him, but this is now so long ago that I will no longer make a secret of the problems I had with this Leica.

Dear fellow photographer, just imagine: off you go with your beloved Leica, through Hungary, Yugoslavia, Bulgaria, Turkey, seeing all sorts of beautiful and interesting things and faithfully recording it all in pictures. The excitement grows with your experiences in Anatolia, Syria, Mesopotamia and half of Persia. You capture all the wonders of the Orient in your little magic box. You regularly send home the films – thirty one Leica spools full of snapshots – and in Teheran you receive the first pictures back in the mail. You will understand the breathless excitement, the trembling fingers with which I tore open the sizeable registered packet with all its strings and seals – all the Leica shots were unusable.

"Aren't you well?" asked the Consul, as I sank into an armchair, pale and aghast.

How could such a thing be possible? Every single exposure from Bulgaria onwards had a black mark either on the edge or across the middle of the picture!

This was a heavy blow. I had promised the Puch Works that I would bring back "good and interesting photographs" – that was what the pages-thick Indian contract specified.

With the greatest respect, Herr Leitz, how was that to be repaired, here in Persia? My despair, pain and anger knew no bounds. Herr Leitz was in Wetzlar and I was in Teheran – we were separated by five thousand kilometres, which was fortunate for him!

"Tell me the best watchmaker in Teheran!"

They took me to an old Persian in the Lallesar, the main street of Teheran. I took a good look at the shop, then at the Persian and then at his tools. This was where I would take the Leica apart. If I succeeded, then it would only be through endless love and patience such as only I myself could bring to the task.

I began systematically, undoing a dozen screws and removing a few parts. I made drawings and sketches of every step of the process. Then I put it all neatly back together again and tested the mechanism.

Then I began the dismantling process afresh, and this time went a few steps deeper into the works of the Leica, but still found nothing wrong with it. I knew instinctively that I could only proceed with the dismantling a step at a time, so as not to lose my way back, and so I rebuilt the whole thing once again, until the recalcitrant Leica looked as good as new.

Then I took it apart again, going just a little further. Where was the fault? I couldn't find it.

Engineers and modelmakers may smile contemptuously at my finicky efforts and the way I kept dismantling and rebuilding in instalments, but I wasn't a precision engineer: I was just a geography student, and only twenty years old at that.

The waiter from the coffee house nearby brought me dish after dish of coffee, while the Persian at my side worked silently on an old alarm clock. A whole day went by. Where was the fault? Should I keep on searching and delve deeper into the complicated mechanism? No, I reassembled the Leica and went back to the hotel. I was terribly cross, and had it in for God and the whole world, as well as Herr Leitz and myself.

The next day I sat next to the Persian watchmaker again. Street urchins peered in at me through the window. All I wanted to do was hurl the Leica through the glass at their shaven heads.

This would not do! I must be calm, brace myself, have faith and then just love the Leica. I began afresh. Now, how did it go yesterday between Step Two and Step Three? I couldn't remember. So, better only go as far as you did yesterday evening. Just go as far as Step Two and then put it together again.

Now to Step Three. And now – well, dear reader, you've got the picture.

Patience is what you learn in the Orient. The master craftsman at my side was still working on his alarm clock. I wondered what on earth people wanted an alarm clock for. Probably they just liked its ringing.

On the afternoon of the second day the Leica was almost completely dismantled.

On a sheet of paper lay the individual screws, levers, springs, nuts, wheels and the most oddly-shaped little parts. Each part had its own number.

And there was the fault: one of the narrow strips of rubberised fabric on the focal-plane shutter was torn. My dear Herr Leitz, would you believe it?

Now where in Teheran could one come by a narrow strip of thin rubberised fabric? By rummaging through the bazaars? It seemed hopeless to me. There I sat with my Leica laid out in a hundred pieces and those scallywags grinning at me idiotically through the window. Somehow the lads knew that I was stumped. What had it all been for? Si tacuisses philosophus mansisses ... (If you had been silent, you would have remained a philosopher)

I looked out, brooding, on to the dusty Lallesar. A watering cart drove by. I saw the water trickling across the street, saw in my mind's eye water, and more water. The mind sometimes makes odd associations of ideas. Water can be rain ... when it rains you wear a raincoat ... preferably a macintosh. Of course! I had a mac, too. A piece of macintosh fabric – that was the answer.

The Leica worked splendidly with this narrow strip of thin rubberised fabric which I cut out of the sleeve of my mac.

The moral of this story is simple – on such an important trip one should always develop some test exposures. We actually had a developing bath with us, but we had just been too lazy. It's quite difficult to make a complete cock-up of exposure times with black and white film, and anyhow, what could possibly go wrong with a Leica?

In the end, making a mess of one set of photos was not the tragedy it might have been, since I had another camera with me and so did Herbert.

On top of these, we also had a ciné camera, but the results were pretty feeble. Apart from making a couple of practice films, I was a rank amateur in this area, which just goes to show that everything has to be learnt.

The good Zierfandler from the consular cellars had put us in an excellent mood. Farewell, then, Oh lovely Teheran! I shall never forget you, especially the 'Knickerbocker Bar' and a watchmaker's shop on the Lallesar. Now we were alone again in the desert. Alone with our thoughts, our longings, and the tireless little Puch.

But the hand of fate was about to remind us that all good things come to an end. Herbert fell ill, seriously ill. Racked by a high fever, he had already been lashing out wildly all night in the tent.

I tried to encourage him, saying, "It's no use, we have to go on."

There was no question of turning back. Teheran already lay several hundred kilometres behind us. Summoning all his strength, Herbert climbed on to his seat. It was only now when he was ill that I noticed what a good pillion rider I'd had. Now he hung there on the back like a sack of flour. The machine often swerved ominously. It was a good thing that the road was so wide, for the most part as wide as the desert. There's nothing as wide as the desert.

"Herbert! For God's sake, we'll hit the deck!"

He groaned something incomprehensible.

I thought I'd better stop.

Herbert slipped down off the machine and lay stretched out on the ground beside me. We were in a hell of a fix. The next oasis was still about ninety kilometres off, but what use would an oasis have been anyway? Sandfly fever is pernicious and there are no powders or pills to deal with it, at least there were none in those days.

There was no systematic research done on sandfly fever until the Second World War. American criminals volunteered to submit to 'Army medical experiments of the US Surgeon General Office.' The American magazine *Reader's Digest* of June 1948 says of this on page 19: "James Duncan (prisoner for life in the State Penitentiary of New Jersey) was the first to be inoculated with the sandfly fever virus which had caused the death of so many of Rommel's men in the African desert."

The report in *Reader's Digest* does not say what the effects of sandfly fever were on James Duncan, but I can imagine it.

By the way, I find the *Reader's Digest* report rather surprising. Sandfly fever is more of an Asian desert illness. I have spoken to many soldiers from the African campaign, but nobody said anything about sandfly fever. I certainly ought to have heard about it, for I was myself with the Afrika Korps for nearly two years.

Compared with sandfly fever, having malaria is quite pleasant. In order to cope with sandfly fever you need an iron constitution. Were we up to it?

Herbert lay beside the machine in the hot sand. I covered him over with coats and blankets. Then he got hot as hell again, rolled around and threw off all the blankets.

As if that wasn't enough, his *sal-jek* sores broke out. We both had *sal-jek*. These are infected ulcers that eat into the flesh right down to the bone. On average they take a year to heal completely. *Sal-jek* is a Persian word meaning 'one year,' and we actually

| Puncture in the Kavir desert between Teheran and Meshed.

did bring these interesting ulcers back to Europe with us, and were most welcome objects of study for university professors.

On this stage of our journey from Teheran to Duzdab – some two thousand kilometres – we went through a great deal. In the normal way of things, we ought to have perished miserably.

A few days later the pernicious sandfly fever laid hold of me, too. I felt as if my skull were full of hot molten lead. The optic nerves were affected and I saw everything through a red haze. Far off, everything was a mess of bloody purple.

We often fell off and stayed lying there for hours. Once a Persian came by and helped us up. I was so feeble and was trembling so much that I was totally unable to pour petrol from the reserve drum into the main tank. The Persian helped me do it, then I just sank back into the roadside ditch. Thinking was a terrible effort, but sometimes I saw in my mind's eye that grave in Kermanshah where Walter Tonn had made his last stop on the road to India.

No, no, no, the blood seemed to hammer through my brain.

Somehow we managed to pull ourselves together and ride on. I can't explain how, but we did. We ate nothing, sometimes drank nothing for a whole day and then frantically lapped up another salty puddle. We seemed to be becoming less than human, but we rode on and on, as if in a dream, because we felt that it was only by constantly moving that we would beat the crisis. If we lay down, we were lost. Somehow, almost unconsciously, we even took a few photographs.

I have six thick volumes filled with newspaper reports of the 1933 India Expedition, but I never wrote anything in the press about this, the greatest crisis of our trip, and I scarcely said a word about it even to our closest friends. Today, I can reveal the reason why I did not. When I returned from the India trip in December 1933, I was already bursting with ideas for new projects, so I told myself that, if anybody found out what a narrow squeak we'd had, and that we'd come through with more luck than judgement, then we would be unlikely to find another company chairman willing to sink quantities of money into a new expedition. ("Well, he said himself it was only by chance that he got to India after all ... ")

I didn't want ideas like that flying about, and so I always made light of it. On the occasion of our first appearance at the Urania Hall, one newspaper wrote " ... he put himself forward in a casual and humorous manner, talking about his trip to India as if it had been an outing down the road to Schwechat."

Today, I can freely admit that this 'outing' was the high point of my life. No subsequent journey provided anything like the same elation, exciting adventures or dangerous moments, the main reason being that by then I had a much better grasp of the skills and knowledge necessary for travel. But on the trip to India I was only twenty years old, and that was the enthralling thing.

Only the powers above know how we came to be spared and reached the little mission station at Meshed. There, they carried us inside like two bundles of misery while the faithful motorcycle stood in the yard, orphaned and abandoned.

What takes only a few minutes to read here lasted in reality for many weeks. I have been unable to give you such a detailed picture of this part of the journey as you might have wished, simply because this great crisis took us so close to the next world. There are borders with the hereafter which no pen can describe.

Sandfly fever and hallucinations. The sun is nearly at the zenith. In spite of the 50°C heat and our overcoats, we are feeling cold and have improvised a sunshade. Have we gone crazy? At each stop, we usually took turns to lie in the shade of the motorcycle – there wasn't enough space for both. How we continued to hoist ourselves up, time and again, to wobble on through the desert now seems almost inexplicable.

Between Teheran and Duzdab, a stretch of 2000km. Sandfly fever, a typical Persian illness, gave us a lot of trouble. Persians contemplate us with indifference, unable to help. People at home had warned us constantly that we would perish along the way.

The missionaries looked after us and got us well again, except for the *sal-jek* sores which take a whole year to heal; and then came the day when, full of hesitation and expectancy, I felt able to set my foot to the kick-starter.

Together again, dear little motorcycle! If it had any idea how much it meant to us! I believe it did know, and was overjoyed to have us back. Fate was being kind to our bike too, kinder than to Walter Tonn's Indian-Mabeco in Kermanshah. So, I thought, sing us your steely song again, carry us onward, on to the south, on to our heart's desire at the end of the trail. Now, thank Heaven, we were back in the saddle. The sandfly fever had been a bad business.

The American missionaries also deserve some recognition. They probably saved our lives. All the same, they didn't inspire any great affection in us. When we fell off the motorcycle at their door we were tatterered and unkempt, and adorned with burns, fever blisters and *sal-jek* boils. The remaining parts of our body were covered with sweat and filth. Our beards had grown rapidly, as they only grow on corpses.

If only our mothers had seen us like that! They would have fainted away, and our fathers would have said, "How could we know the young scamps were that crazy?"

But our parents were far off, almost a world away. Only the missionaries were there. American missionaries, be they Baptists, Methodists, Presbyterians, Anglicans or members of one of the many American sects, are mostly very sharp business people. Reverend H of the Meshed mission was exceptionally sharp. We had scarcely ceased to look like wild animals and regained our human shape, when he came fishing for information. Had we any money to pay for our care? It cost so much per day, plus bed and medication.

This rankled with us terribly – not because of the money, but because of the attitude. The way we saw it, it was as if a dairyman up on the alp at home had rescued an American tourist who had got into difficulties while climbing, and as soon as he got him to the mountain hut, asked him how much he could pay.

Reverend H was certainly a good doctor. He may also have been a good missionary, but he hadn't an ounce of feeling in him.

We paid him everything in good American dollars, and much joy may it have brought him. We were truly indebted to him for taking us in at all at his mission in the back of beyond, for when we knocked on his door, we really did not look as if we had any money to spend. The admirable Reverend H ran a considerable risk in taking us in. He was actually a man of courage!

Herbert later had a second encounter with the Reverend H which he told me about a few years later in Vienna. When taking our leave in Meshed the time before, we had felt moved to make a number of unkind remarks to him: how we thought he was a very bad Christian, how we would write all about him for the American newspapers whose special correspondents we were, and how we would naturally avoid entering his inhospitable house a second time. The missionary did not seem particularly upset by any of these observations. No doubt he considered himself far better placed than we were to judge Christian or un-Christian behaviour, and anyway, we did not give the impression of being special correspondents for American newspapers. As for our final threat of never looking him up in the future, he only heaved a sigh of relief and said, "I hope not!"

Three years later Herbert came through Meshed again on a motorcycle. He was coming from Afghanistan on his way home. He was healthy, did not have sandfly fever, and was thoroughly resolved on giving the mission a wide berth. But, man proposes, God disposes. This time Herbert, apparently master of his fate, was steering badly. He ended up running into deep sand with the motorcycle somewhere beyond Herat and fell off, burning a piece of flesh off his leg on the hot exhaust pipe. The wound was painful and swollen, and, to cut a long story short, Herbert was only too happy to discover in Meshed a competent, if somewhat unfriendly medical missionary.

It was late evening when he arrived at the mission station. He was looking just as dusty as we had the time before. He rang the doorbell and waited. He heard heavy steps coming and knew it was the American himself. Asians tread much more softly. The door opened and there was the American glaring at him.

"Ah," he said, "here you are again. So you didn't keep your promise."

"But I've got money," said Herbert, holding out to him an American ten-dollar-bill. You could live for a long time in Persia then on such a sum, and Herbert expected him to accept it with pleasure.

But the missionary indignantly refused the money, saying firmly, "I take no money!"

He then treated Herbert and still wouldn't take money, in spite of having bound up his leg with a large quantity of clean bandages.

On parting, he said, "When your friend comes through here, I guess he'll be sick too, so tell him to come straight to me."

I wonder what brought about this strange transformation. However, I was unable to make use of his invitation, as I had already passed through Meshed one year previously on the Steyr world trip without visiting him, and was actually in America when he issued this 'invitation' via Herbert. Perhaps he knew.

Enough of that. Meshed is a wonderful town. In spite of the weakness remaining in our limbs, we took full delight in this, the greatest shrine in Persia, before we left. Imam Reza, a disciple of Ali, the adopted son of Mohammed, is buried here. The relationship is somewhat tenuous, but Imam Reza is nevertheless one of the greatest saints of Shi'ite Islam. The domes of his mosque are gilded and shine far out into the desert. I wanted to take a picture of this glorious building, but I came close to being done to death.

Over a hundred thousand pilgrims come annually from all parts of the Shi'ite world to Meshed. These people have little sympathy for a roumi, an infidel, who traps their holy shrine in a picture box and carries it off.

Probably the pilgrims would have killed me if I had not presented such a pitiful spectacle. I was so thin my bones were showing, with my mournful eyes still full of sandfly fever and my face so covered with *sal-jek* boils, it scarcely seemed worth it. So they dragged me to the police station and there the film was ripped from my camera. Thank you very much. I was already halfway to being an Oriental, bearing all these insults with stoic calm. They could have their old mosque back. (Two years later on the car journey across Asia, I did photograph it after all.)

This Meshed is a mighty town on the edge of the desert. Seventy thousand inhabitants live within its walls. How do they make their living? From pilgrims, exactly as in Mecca, Karbala, Kum and Isfahan, and other centres of Islamic culture.

Meshed also produces magnificent carpets and silk velvets, and nowhere have I seen more beautiful gold and jewel work than in the bazaars there. I often wished that our travel funds could have run to buying all these lovely things. Then there were the weapons. Skilled smiths and enthusiastic merchants spread before us an unimaginable variety of magnificent hand-made weapons. What imagination these Orientals have! We in the West are mean-minded orphan children by comparison.

It is a fact that in Arabic, for the word 'sword' alone, in its manifold forms and various uses there exist eight hundred and fifty different words! There you have the proverbial richness of Oriental language. To take another example: there are about two hundred different expressions for the concept 'hill.' Every sort of hill has its own definition, depending on steepness, point of the compass, vegetation, how easy it is to walk on, and many other points of distinction.

Can such a language be learned? I did try. Armed with Herder's *Arab Grammar*, I attended evening classes at the consular academy in Vienna. They said I was a very good student and praised the progress I made. The results in practice were shattering: not a soul understood me.

In each country we picked up the most important words in the street. The sad thing was that we always had to leave the country just as we had managed to learn a little of the language, and then the trouble would begin all over again.

In the big cities people usually understand French and English, and on the road one has to get by with sign language and a few odd words picked up here and there.

In Meshed we got our tanks filled up again. The Anglo-Iranian Oil company had given us a splendid letter of introduction to all its depots in Persia. This letter was a unique document. It was divided vertically in two: on the left was the text in English

Meshed in Eastern Persia, the great city of pilgrimage. This first aerial photo is from 1933. In the centre lies the complex with the tomb and mosque of Imam Reza.

and on the right in Persian. The Persian text was written with an Arabic typewriter. Such a thing exists. The Arab alphabet consists of twenty-eight letters which are all consonants. Vowels are not written, rather as in stenography with us.

Persia is not a single unit. Apart from Persians, the country is also home to ethnic Turks, Kurds, Baluchis, Turkmens, and Arabs.

The Golden Mosque of Imam Reza in Meshed on the Persian-Afghan frontier where the distinguished modern Persian poet Firdusi lived for a long time.

# 10
# OUR LIFE IN THE DESERT

In Meshed we made a right-angled turn southwards, and, as we travelled south, the landscape changed imperceptibly. It is hard to describe the difference. There were the same huge bare mountains and the grey ribbon of road through the grey desert, just as on the way from Teheran to Meshed, but up there you saw the occasional snow-covered peak to the north, and sometimes the light green shimmer of thin grass or perhaps the dark green fringe of a forest. There was not much vegetation but just enough to let us hope for something new round the next corner, the sight of a real forest, maybe, or a flowery meadow where we could lie down for a bit.

The five hundred kilometres from Meshed to Birjand, through Torbat-e-Heydarieh, Jugman and Qayen is one of the most mountainous I have ever travelled. Five hundred kilometres through the passes of the Dolomites are a mere nothing compared with this.

Any expectation of forest or meadows now seemed totally ridiculous. There had never been any grass or trees here; nor would there ever be any. There was only sand and stones and dry earth. Besides this, this landscape made a mockery of all the rules we were familiar with. We find it normal for smaller valleys to lead into a larger valley which slowly decreases in altitude until it debouches into yet another one. There is nothing resembling a valley system here: in fact, it is the particular characteristic of these mountains to have no system at all. Because these mountains have always been arid, there are no rivers, nor any valleys that can be followed. Instead, the traveller is faced with a jumble of mountains, criss-crossing his path at random. It is all up and down, often with vertiginous climbs of far more than one in three, which bear no comparison with our classic climb up the Katschberg in Austria.

The caravans get over this without a problem, but it made the highest demands on our valiant Puch. The engine often overheated, we often got off and pushed, and we often feared that all of our combined strength would not be enough.

It may have been some small consolation to our faithful machine to be surrounded by people whenever we halted at a Persian oasis. Here, the clean-up routine was completed without difficulty, since the strange vehicle was explored all over wherever the human hand could reach. What a wondrous race are the Persians! Their joyful child-like curiosity soon made us forget all our tribulations. They were particularly taken with the lovely red-enamelled Tyrolean eagle which I had mounted on the petrol cap as a mascot. They couldn't keep their fingers off it, and it really is a miracle that the Tyrolean eagle stood up to all that pulling and tugging.

During the Second World War the Tyrolean eagle and the motorcycle with it lay in safe keeping in the Technical Museum in Vienna. It remained under the museum's protection throughout the confused years of the Occupation, when some Russian or American might well have taken a fancy to such an unusual machine. My sincere thanks are due to the head of the Mechanical Engineering Department, Hofrat Dr Seper. These days I have the India Puch at home with me. It stands in my garage alongside eighteen other veterans. As anyone will understand, this motorcycle is my favourite, and the one I carefully maintain and keep in running order. It has to start on the first kick, as I have often claimed (and won bets with some who wouldn't believe me!) I ride out on the India Puch several times a year and it simply changes my outlook. As I like to say on returning from these excursions, "It keeps me young!"

Apart from the Tyrolean eagle, the Persians were particularly fascinated by the thick foam rubber covering the saddles. They were forever trying it out, full of wonder and amazement. They fired hundreds of barely comprehensible questions at us about the foam rubber alone. When we couldn't take any more from people, we photographed them and this cowed them into a respectful silence. They froze like pillars of salt.

There was another Austrian en route from Meshed to southern Persia at the same time as we were. Together with his wife, Dr Gabriel was travelling by camel caravan through the Lut desert, and had already been on the move for about twenty days. He was travelling parallel to us, but a good hundred kilometres over to westward. There was no way of making contact with him, since caravans travel only at night, and it was not until sunset that the caravanserais came to life, just as we would be pitching our tent.

We were already four hours ahead by the clock compared with European time, and every morning as we made our machine ready to go in the first rays of the rising sun, we had the satisfaction of knowing that all our friends back home were still lazing in bed.

This is how we started the day: having spent all night snug in the tent, we were awoken by the cool of the morning, and one of us would crawl outside and take a sniff at the new day. Sometimes we would see tracks around our camping place which had not been there the previous evening. They were the tracks of hyenas, jackals or wild donkeys. These were all harmless beasts. Mostly we did not even hear them, so deep and untroubled were our slumbers. As for robbers or bandits, there may well have been a few in these lonely areas of eastern Persia, but none of them had a go at us. It would scarcely have been worth their while, in any case.

Apart from these, the other main danger in the desert was scorpions. These delightful creatures grow in Persia to about fourteen centimetres long and retaliate viciously if you are so careless as to crawl out of the tent with bare feet and tread on the tail of one. The attack is not deadly, but it is pretty nasty. The Persians always say that you can drive a scorpion to commit suicide. If you just take a burning-glass and burn him quite hard on the head, then he gets in such a fury that he stings himself in the back with his tail and dies. I have heard this several times in Persia. It is not very probable, since I know for a fact that the venom of certain Indian snakes has no harmful effect on the creatures themselves.

There is also said to be a little blue louse, which we never got to see, although we saw hundreds of other lice, bugs and fleas. Its bite is said to be lethal in every case. We were told about it so often and so insistently that we developed an unspoken aversion to anything blue. A solicitous girlfriend in the Tyrol had sewn the seams of my sleeping bag together especially tightly, "So it doesn't tear open and send all the feathers flying around the desert," she said, but she had used blue thread. Seldom can a well-intentioned act have been rewarded with such crass ingratitude! Many were the shrieks of terror emitted by Herbert or myself on awaking after a dream-filled night during which we had been menaced by advancing legions of blue lice, only to see the dreaded creatures actually marching in a straight line up my sleeping bag, right at my face! There were always a couple of agonising moments before we remembered the blue thread and inwardly cursed the girl who had sewn up the sleeping bag, for all that she had done it with the best intentions! I had once told her that blue was my favourite colour (she had blue eyes), but that was back in the Tyrol where they have blue rivers, blue sky and blue eyes but absolutely no blue lice.

But I was meaning to tell you about getting started in the morning. The first one up would fetch the little spade from the machine and stroll off into the desert. We called this 'going for a dig.' It was always an eagerly awaited event, since a regular bowel habit is a good indicator of general health.

Meeting up with a caravan which had a very different pattern of travel from ours. In summer the caravans travel by night and rest up by day. We did the opposite, because of finding our way. If we parked the motorcycle far enough away from the resting caravan and approached on foot, we were welcomed as guests. On the left is a caravanserai built by Shah Abbas about 300 years ago. The whole of Persia was provided with caravanserais. Today most are in ruins.

The tent on the Sahara trip was too big – it weighed too much! Every half-kilo had to be saved on the India expedition, hence this tiny tent, seen here outside a Persian village where the inn was not very inviting. We were afraid of the notorious 'blue lice' of Persia.

Then we would pack up the tent and strap it on to the machine. For the first time that morning we would sigh and get into a sweat. There was no water, of course, which meant no washing. Often we did not wash for days, and stank like musk oxen. Breakfast would have been nice, but usually we didn't have the necessary on board. Anyway, every minute counted if we were to make the most of the cool of the morning for travelling, so we rode off on an empty stomach until the heat forced us to get off the machine. We would rest over midday at a Persian tea-house on the caravan route, wherever we could find one. If not, we made do with the shade of a tamarisk or a rock or the shade of our own machine. In the teahouses, the chai-chanees, we would eat tough chicken, greasy mutton shanks and juicy watermelons. Sometimes we even cleaned our teeth. Shaving we gave up as a bad job.

In the chai-chanees we would get them to brew us lots of green tea and took it with us in our water tanks between stopping places. The fluid needs of the human body – for Europeans at least – are very great. You need three to five litres of water every day. Only a little of this goes through the usual channels: most of it is lost by sweating.

That was how we lived in the desert, because we were young and did not need the approval of civilisation, and because our eyes were set on our final goal, the wonderland of India. Nothing is achieved by fussing over trivialities.

# 11
# LETTERS FROM HOME

In Birjand, halfway between Meshed and Duzdab, we stopped off for two days. The town of Birjand lies near to the Afghan border and can thus boast a branch of the Persian State Bank *Banque Emeli*. It was to the manager of this bank, Effendi Badi Massud, that we carried a recommendation giving us the power to draw Persian money on a letter of credit. We always avoided carrying large sums of cash with us, and travelled with cheques and letters of credit.

One would be quite wrong in thinking that Middle Eastern countries do not possess an organised banking system. The Persian State Bank, for example, has been developed by Austrian experts, and the manager of the head office in Teheran was Herr Gold, a Viennese.

In other large Persian cities, too, there were Austrians working as managers for the Persian State Bank. In smaller towns the bank employed Persian officials, but whether they were foreigners or Persians, we generally found these bank officials to be interesting, educated people who were able to tell us much about the land and its people, and to whom in return we were able to recount the details of our journey. In this way we passed many delightful hours with our kind hosts.

We only had one unusual experience, and that was in Kermanshah, the first moderate-sized town we came to in Persia. Here, too, we had business at the bank – several forms we had been given at the border had to be endorsed or given a visa – anyway, we had to go to the bank. It was afternoon when we arrived and we were informed that the manager, a German gentleman, had already gone home. We were welcome to look for him there, so that is what we did. He received us in a friendly manner, took charge of our customs documents and said that the business would be attended to the following morning when his clerks were on duty again, if we would just be at the bank at ten o'clock. We agreed happily and drank the delicious coffee he had set before us. Now, in small Asian towns such as this, there is rarely an inn that is even halfway acceptable to Europeans, and we had rather taken it for granted that the bank manager would invite us to spend the night at his house, the more so as he led a very solitary existence here. So we waited. To begin with we were looking forward to enjoying the evening, then our confidence waned, until finally we felt only panic. It was already dark and still the manager had said nothing to relieve our fears.

At last I asked, "Where can we find a bed here in Kermanshah?"

"I don't know the inns," said the bank manager, "but I'm sure you'll find something suitable."

"Our experience of local inns has been rather unpleasant," I said. "We'd prefer to sleep in our tent."

"If you go north," said the bank manager, "you'll soon be on the open steppe and it's not too far for you to come back tomorrow."

We rode north and put up our tent. We had been thinking that a sort of brotherhood existed among white men in Asia and we were so surprised by this inhospitable attitude for which we could see no explanation. "The man is mad," we said, and went off to sleep.

The next morning, he was kindness itself. Would we take lunch with him? We would, as we hadn't had any breakfast. Would we stay another night in Kermanshah? We would not. We said our campsite had been quite nice, but by no means so enchanting that we wanted to spend a second night there.

At this, the bank manager gave an embarrassed laugh. "Had we found his behaviour the day before rather odd?" We said that indeed we had. He said that he regretted it most deeply, but only late that night had he learned via a telephone conversation with the customs post that we were carrying a letter of recommendation from the Persian ambassador in Berlin, and that we really *were* Austrian students on a minor world trip, and not unemployed layabouts on the scrounge. He had recently had an unfortunate experience with one of these, a solid, respectable-looking chap from Hamburg. He had turned up just as we had done, and of course had been invited to stay the night. He had stayed not just one night, but three weeks and had then suddenly disappeared, along with any valuables he could carry. The bank manager had not approached the police about it, since the man from Hamburg had been seen as a personal friend and he feared that the Persians might gain a very unfavourable impression of German friendship thereby. He begged our comprehension and forgiveness. This we gave, and over a bottle of Moselle (the bank manager being from the Rhineland), we celebrated our reconciliation.

As we never knew exactly where our predecessor from Hamburg had already stopped off, we always took extreme care henceforth to declare ourselves from the outset as harmless students. We had planned to do the same in Birjand, but this was unnecessary.

If Birjand had not been a rather pathetic settlement that had only acquired the designation of a town because of the sparseness of population in desert areas, then the entry we made there could only have been described as princely. We were riding through the desert with not a soul to be seen, when a few flatroofed houses came into view. There were more of them than appeared at first sight, since they were the same colour as the desert and could only be recognised as houses when we came near enough to them. We got ready to ask for the *Banque Emeli*, and had our question prepared and fluent. At the entrance to the town stood two dignified Persians, who bowed deeply as we approached. We bowed in return, and because Herbert bowed out to the right-hand side in order not to bump his nose on my back, we nearly lost our balance and I had a job to keep the bike on the road. Then I saw that the Persians were pointing forward in a solemn and inviting manner. The road ahead of us was full of people. Don't get me wrong, it wasn't like the crush in a bazaar or the crowds gathered to welcome Lindbergh or Eisenhower on Fifth Avenue in New York, but just a few peasants peering at us in an embarrassed way and a few women, although we could not tell whether they were peering at us or not, since they were veiled. However, for Birjand it *was* like Lindbergh arriving in New York, and our hearts missed a beat as we realised that we were the main attraction. There was no point in denying it out of false modesty, Birjand had a magnificent welcome planned for us. Sure enough, at the next street corner stood two policemen, and while one held the people back against the wall, the other pointed the way for us, with another bow. So we came at last, bowing all the time, to the house of the bank manager. There at the open door stood two servants in blue uniforms, again making gestures of invitation and directing us on. At last we met Badi Massud. He was smiling broadly.

"They told me in Teheran that you were coming, and people in Birjand have never seen a motorcycle, so the police chief and I decided to create a slight sensation with your arrival. The summer here is very boring."

Dear, good Badi Massud. Not only did he create a sensation for the people of Birjand, but also for us with his unsurpassed hospitality. He let us do exactly as we liked, just saying by way of explanation, "You can sleep here on this flat roof, where it is coolest. Here is the bathroom. Here you will find German books and newspapers. And of course the garden is at your disposal all day and all night."

The garden was surrounded by a high wall. In it stood many pomegranate trees full of split, overripe fruit, from which the gaudy red pips twinkled. We lay in this garden on our backs in the soft grass and dreamed of home. It is wonderful on a journey like this to do nothing for a change except gaze up at the sky, reviewing all your great experiences in your mind's eye, and marvelling at the power of the Almighty.

We only saw Badi Massud at mealtimes. With perfect sensitivity, he left us to indulge our idleness in his garden. He himself had studied for many years in Germany, and had a pretty good idea of how we were feeling. From time to time he sent a servant with a tray of Persian pastries and a pot of tea. He was a subscriber to the *Frankfurter Allgemeine Zeitung* and our hungry minds eagerly devoured the editions of the last few months. How beautiful it was in Badi Massud's green garden!

Then I set about opening all our mail. The last time we had received letters was in Teheran. Here was a letter from my mother, full of anxiety and longing, and some lines from my father with advice and admonition; then a letter from Steyr-Daimler-Puch AG with replies to the technical enquiries we had sent them, closing with some very fine words of praise and encouragement with all good wishes for our ultimate success. This did a lot for our spirits. The Shell Motor Oil Company in London sent us directions for our fuel supplies in India. How we wished we were there already!

Several letters from Susanne had arrived at once. She had registered me for the new semester, and Herr Vukovich, the college porter, had helped her convince the professors who were being difficult. If I returned by Christmas, I would not have to repeat the semester, but I would have to work really hard to catch up on all I had missed. The crammer tutor who held court at the *Hochschule* café was ready to prepare me for the exams with a crash course. That was splendid.

There was one annoying letter from my landlady, Frau Pawel. She wrote that she could no longer keep my room for me, and that I should authorise someone to come and collect my belongings. Since her daughter had got a contract at the *Rosenhügel* (a film studio in Vienna), she was not letting rooms any more. This was terribly sad. I imagined getting back to Vienna when all this was over, probably having a laurel wreath put round my neck, being photographed, filmed, bombarded with questions, and then, when the party was over, not knowing where I would lay my head that night. After my first night back (in a hotel) I would have to take the tram out to the college and study all the accommodation advertisements on the notice board in the main hall. The distant prospect of Europe was a sad one, and I began to dread my return.

My pile of post also contained an official communication. Frau Pawel had kindly dealt with it and paid the excess postage. It was from the police station in Wieden and was the usual sort of traffic penalty, *viz*, for riding a motorcycle along the *Favoritenstrasse* at 14.40 hours on 17 June 1933 whilst removing my jacket.

This was probably quite correct. If you get too hot on a heavy summer day in Vienna, you do take off your jacket, even riding along on a motorcycle. It must be admitted that both arms must be free in order to slip out of the sleeves, and so you do have to ride a little way with no hands. What is so strange in that?

The traffic cop who watched me perform this operation apparently did find it somewhat strange, and reported me. Result: a fine of 20 *Schilling*, or in case of non-feasibility, twelve hours detention. Both options were 'non-feasible' for the moment. Neither I nor the 20 *Schilling* were available, since I was lying in Badi Massud's garden in eastern Persia, and it was rather a long way to Vienna. The police station in Wieden would have to wait patiently till I returned, with the promise that I would turn up and begin my sentence. It wouldn't be the first time.

In the past I had collected several tickets for illegal parking, or allegedly exceeding the speed limit. As a student I had always regarded paying fines as an unnecessary expense, so I would tuck a couple of textbooks under my arm and report in for detention. At least it gave you time to study in peace for the next exam.

Every time they would go through the pantomime of taking away my belt so that I couldn't commit suicide, and shut me in a cell. It was great to have time to myself for once, and to be obliged to get on with my much-needed studies. But I ended up being too clever by half – literally by half, because when it came to the middle of the day and the other inmates got their lunch, the warder came in grinning and said they hadn't cooked for me as I was going home at half time. I was speechless, but apparently I had got remission for 'good behaviour' and was free to go now. What rotten luck! Just when I really wanted to do some studying. Was it a crime, then, to want to study in peace for once? So there I was out on the street again, but I managed to get something to eat in the college canteen.

I sat out many a sentence in this way. Don't imagine that I was some sort or motorbike hooligan. Far from it. But the State needed money and was very quick on the draw with penalties for 'infractions of the traffic regulations,' either cash down, or in the case of 'non-feasibility' with detention in the cells. The Treasury didn't make much money out of me, so it is understandable that its generosity did not run to feeding me as well. I soon realised this, and, if I were a bit short of time already, I would not report for detention until eleven o'clock in the morning, and then I would be free again at noon.

It's not as if I didn't have the money to pay a 20 *Schilling* fine, but going through all the ceremonial of being locked up every time was such a lark. Not that my financial situation *in statu pupillari* looked exactly rosy. My father had dispatched me to Vienna in order to pursue the noble calling of an architect, but during the first two semesters it gradually dawned on me that geography held considerably more interest, so I changed courses. Being the idiot I was at that age, I said nothing about it at home. I had been on the books of the University Department of World Trade for a whole year before Father found out by chance that his darling boy had ditched architecture a long time back. Father did not mince words in giving his verdict. "You changed courses without telling me; now see how you get along on your own."

Of course, it was a blow to be suddenly deprived of my usual 200 *Schilling* a month, but I have already explained how I made out as a film courier in Vienna, which was almost better than when Father was footing the bill.

It seems strange that I thought so much about prison in Vienna, there in Birjand where policemen couldn't even write and would bow so low before me that their caps nearly fell off.

It's a funny thing about those Persian caps. They look rather like French policemen's caps, with a high crown and a deep peak in front. Reza Shah seemed to have given them the status of a national headdress. Everybody had to wear one. The cunning Shah had a very definite aim in that he was trying to break the power of the *mullahs*, the Moslem clerics. He did not dare take action against them openly; the example of his eastern colleague, the King of Afghanistan, who had lost both his throne and his country because of over-hasty reforms, was reason enough to proceed cautiously. The cap served the purpose. When at prayer, Moslems must touch the ground with the forehead, and they must carry out their prayers with the head covered. This was impossible when wearing a cap *à la* Reza Shah, since the large peak prevented the forehead from touching the ground. The Shah probably thought that if prayers could not be said properly any more, then the *mullahs* would soon lose the great influence they exerted. But pious Persians found a solution which insulted neither the commandments of Allah or of Reza Shah, and it was such a simple one. They turned the cap through 180 degrees, so that the peak stuck out over the back, allowing them to press their forehead to the earth as hard as they liked. In the evening after the final prayers of the day, we would often see forgetful old gentlemen with their caps back to front, strolling contentedly through the streets. They would get stern looks from policemen and, feeling guilty and embarrassed, they would turn their headgear round again.

But I am way off the point. I was wondering why I thought so often of my old prison experiences back in Vienna while I was in Birjand. It was nothing to do with policemen, but with Badi Massud's garden. There is something peculiar and symbolic about gardens in the desert, locked away from the outside world behind a high wall, not like any of the walls we know in Europe, but a mud wall several metres high. It shuts out all views and smothers all sound. There is one world outside the wall and another within, exactly as in a gaol, except that here it is the other way round. The world outside the wall is miserable, dreary and poverty-stricken, a wilderness of heat and sand, and the world inside is a paradise with splashing fountains, little trickling brooks laid out in artful twists and turns through the garden, lush green grass below and green trees above with brilliant red pomegranates. This was the garden where we lay after riding several thousand kilometres through the desert, and read the *Frankfurter Allgemeine Zeitung*! Birjand and Badi Massud are inscribed in gold in my diary.

Two letters had arrived from my friend Detoni. Detoni was my journalistic nursemaid. To him I sent the reports of the trip, just as I dashed them off, any old how, and he would fine-tune them, duplicate them and pass them on to the newspapers with whom I had contracts. He was my mentor, supporter and friend, and I have him to thank for spurring me on, time and again, to turn my plans into reality. It was he who made me a member of the *Europa Motor Tourist* club. As a division of the Austrian Touring Club, it brought together all motorists who were interested in long journeys. I read about it quite by chance in a Vienna newspaper and applied straight away, even though at that time I did not have any special achievement to my name apart from the journey from Kufstein to Vienna (by train), but I considered myself perfectly well qualified to be accepted as a member. I succeeded, and was given the task of fetching beer from the pub opposite for thirsty club members, and later on in the evening, making hot dogs and coffee. The fact that I really wanted to go to India was set aside as irrelevant. The then president of the club was a Herr Herkner, the proud possessor of a four-cylinder Henderson machine. Of course, this impressed me mightily, since I myself came to the clubhouse every Wednesday evening on the Number 2 tram.

The aforementioned Herr Detoni was secretary of the club and also published a photographic journal, the *Allgemeine Photographische Zeitung*. He was one of only a very few people who did not consider my scheme completely hare-brained. He took me under his wing, slaked my nineteen-year-old thirst for knowledge, and soon found someone else to see to the thirst of the other club members.

The Europa Motor Tourist was only a modest club in itself, but it is it I have to thank for putting me in touch with the gentlemen of the Austrian Automobile Club and the Austrian Touring Club, whose opinions really counted. You can appreciate the significance that these contacts had for me when you consider that I had just enough money in my pocket to pay for a tram fare, yet intended to make a journey to India. I suffered constantly from an inferiority complex. In quiet moments I would often admit to myself that there was no way my resources would ever stretch to the plans I was making. However, I needn't have worried as far as the Automobile Club was concerned. I was amazed at the way it offered me, as a matter of course, access to its wealth of experience, its aids to touring and its connections abroad. I was a member of the club, and apparently that was sufficient reason for it to take me under its wing and support me in word and deed. This was customer service of a very high order, as I now realise, for in spite of all my good intentions, I was still a very dubious customer. I wouldn't be at all surprised if the gentlemen of the Automobile Club entertained serious doubts of my great project ever coming to anything. I can scarcely think too highly of them for never letting me suspect what they thought, and for the tireless way they looked after me.

In the two letters that I perused in Badi Massud's garden, Detoni gave me various pointers to what the European readership found especially interesting, and told me that a string of other newspapers had accepted my accounts of the trip. This was gratifying, not just because of the fees, of course, but mainly because I would be making myself known, and this would open the way to further great projects. It is only today I realise what an endlessly difficult and arduous business it is to make a name for oneself. Leafing through the thick albums of press reports, countless interviews and newspaper discussions, adding to that the seven hundred or so lectures, the innumerable talks on film and all the radio reports, you might suppose that this makes your name known to some extent. Not a bit of it. This is all a drop in the ocean. If newspapers say, 'The well-known explorer Dr Max Reisch is planning such-and-such,' then you're not really well-known. It's only when they start referring to you simply as 'Max Reisch' or just 'Reisch' that you know you've made it. Actually, I never got that far!

In Badi Massud's garden on the Afghan frontier I answered all the letters from home and wrote the report for the last stage of our journey. This could never be put off for very long, since the newspapers were waiting for it. Badi Massud offered to send our letters via Persian business post to Teheran. From there, they would get to Vienna in three or four days on the Junkers aircraft of German-Persian Airlines.

It was a pity we were not allowed into Afghanistan. In spite of insistent warnings from Herr Ehlers, the Consul in Teheran, we had not given up the idea, even though he was convinced that he had dissuaded us. Here in Birjand on the border with Afghanistan we felt our disappointment twice as keenly. The route to India through Afghanistan would have been significantly shorter than through Baluchistan

But it was hopeless. The ban on motorcycles entering the country had remained in place ever since the Stratil-Sauer incident. This concerned a German who had been riding a motorcycle from the Indian direction entering Afghanistan via the Khyber Pass. The din of his engine frightened the horse of an Afridi, who was thrown from the saddle. For a proud tribal warrior, this is about the most shameful experience possible. The man scrambled up and threatened Stratil-Sauer with his shotgun. The German used his revolver and unfortunately his shot proved fatal. The dead man's clan declared a blood-feud, as was usual in Afghanistan. Stratil-Sauer was put in prison in Kabul in order to ensure his safety, but the influential tribe demanded that he be handed over. The Afghan government was in a difficult position. The case was resolved by the courageous action of the Italian Consul who, probably with the full knowledge of the Afghan authorities, stuffed the unfortunate German into a sack and smuggled him out of the country by car. Since then, entry has generally been forbidden to noisy motorbikes. Only from 1936 could exceptional permission be granted, and then only seldom. In 1933 we were obliged to make the detour through Baluchistan. We felt a holy awe as we faced this inferno of sand and sun, and our premonitions of evil were to prove true. Baluchistan nearly cost us our happy-go-lucky lives.

We spent two days with Badi Massud in Birjand, and it was hard saying goodbye to him, and to his quiet garden with its lush green grass and glut of pomegranates, but it couldn't be helped. We saddled our trusty metal steed and rode out into the desert, silent and heavy-hearted. Now and then I looked back and exchanged glances with Herbert. Then, without a word from either of us, I turned the machine round and rode back to Birjand, through the big gate and straight into Badi Massud's green garden. All we wanted was the pleasure of one more day in that dreamland paradise before the desert took us in its grip. Badi Massud greeted us effusively like old friends whom he had been longing to see for years, although it was only an hour ago that we had said goodbye to him. We spent another whole day lying in his garden, reading the letters from home over and over again.

I wished that we could stay in the garden for ever, we were so happy there. All the same, western feelings of responsibility began to stir in us. What would the management at Steyr-Daimler-Puch AG say if we wrote and told them that we had taken employment with Badi Massud as his gardeners?

No, it wouldn't do. We stayed another day because Badi Massud said we were still looking very weak after our sandfly fever. He said this and we were only too ready to believe him.

We had to conquer our weaker selves. We simply couldn't be spongers for ever, lying around in other peoples' gardens. We promised Badi Massud that we would write to him often when we got back to Europe. Alas, we never did. This is a sad thing. On trips like this one gets to know so many interesting people who deserve thanks, and one has every intention of writing them kind letters or sending them a little something at Christmas, but these good intentions are rarely acted upon and when it comes down to it, the traveller is a thoroughly ungrateful human being.

# 12

# THE SALT DESERT OF DASHT-E-LUT

From Birjand to Hormuk, the way extended for four hundred kilometres through the wilderness of Dasht-e-Lut. We were riding along the Afghan border directly north to south. 'Along the border' is a relative term, since for the most part we were still a hundred kilometres distant from it, although a hundred scarcely signifies in a country where kilometres are reckoned in thousands.

Life on Persian country roads has a charm all its own. No matter how great the distances that we covered, whether in the mountains of Kurdistan or on the desert plain of Lut in shimmering heat, we met with the same scenes and the same characters. The prevailing impression was that the country was going over more and more to motor traffic and that the camel, which had dominated the roads for thousands of years, was losing its place. Two years later, I came through Persia again, and by then the process was complete. Ancient caravanserais, which at the time of our motorcycle trip were still a cross between garage and caravanserai, had, in the space of two years, converted entirely to motor traffic, and a camel would have seemed as out of place there as in the middle of Vienna. However, my knowledge of those days extends only to the main-road traffic, and the camel will no doubt last longer on the by-roads. But camel owners were facing an uncertain future, and whenever we stopped to mend a puncture or do some repairs, people came and offered us camels for sale. Foreigners passing through on a two-wheeled car would surely be daft enough to do anything: they might even buy a camel.

The voice of the camel seller who had been besieging me for an hour in an attempt to sell me one of his camels began to wheedle, "*Sarkar* (Lord), may your shadow never grow less, but truly, seventy *toman* for this camel which is swifter than the wind and more tenacious than the eagle, it is not a great sum."

Only a few years previously the price of a camel varied between 100 and 200 *toman* and good animals were usually hard to come by, but now the price had sunk to less than half what it had been. Camels, denizens of the lonely caravan roads of Persia for thousands of years, are now, slowly but surely, being superseded by the automobile, which is now on the point of conquering the Middle East. It was not until just after the Great War that the tracks trodden into the hard earth of the desert by thousands of camels' feet began to be improved and the road system extended. Shah Pahlevi realised the importance of roads in a land which lacked railways, and, thanks to his initiative, Persia today possesses nine thousand kilometres of first-class roads, and seven thousand kilometres of inferior tracks, which can, nevertheless, take motor vehicles. However, road building in Persia is made easier by the extreme hardness of the ground. In places, all that is needed is to clear a few rocks out of the way and level off the ground a bit, and there you have a really good road. On the other hand, the mountain passes at up to three thousand metres altitude present a huge challenge to the engineer, and some of these roads, like the Assadabad pass, are bold constructions without precedent. The way Persians drive is evidence of the fatalism which typifies their race. They hurtle round the dangerous bends at alarming speed, and many an upturned wreck marks the site of a catastrophe. But the driver never takes this as a warning, since his *kismet*, the destiny which Allah has appointed for him, will be fulfilled whether he drives fast or slowly.

"Tomorrow evening I shall be in Teheran, *inshallah*," he thinks. This *inshallah* – if God wills – is added to every instance of the future tense in Persian, for how can one go against the will of Allah? It makes far more sense to say your morning and evening prayers diligently than to replace your brake blocks.

However little a Persian has of anything, he always has time. For this reason, motor traffic in this country is relatively sparse. Many ride on their tiny donkeys and ignore the motors. Passengers are carried in small lorries. The back part of the lorry is shut in with wire netting like a sort of cage, with a few rugs on the floor as the only concession to comfort. It is quite incredible how many people can be fitted into one of these cages.

There was great excitement in the caravanserai as the bus was due to leave in a few minutes. First, a few women got in, chattering. They climbed nimbly inside without lifting their *chador* in the process. Then the men got in. A soldier who watched me as I took a photograph, gave me a friendly nod, saying, "*Cheili chub*," (very good). Now the cage was really full, but a few men were still trying to squeeze themselves in. The last one succeeded with a great effort in getting one hand wedged in the middle of the lorry – try as he might, there was no room for more. Then two helpers came to his aid, grasped the hand, pushed and pulled till the sweat ran down their faces. This grim and silent struggle lasted for several minutes, then there was a sudden jerk and the man disappeared into the middle of the lorry. Two planks were quickly pushed across the opening at the back to prevent any passenger from falling out, and the lorry roared off, never stopping until it came to the next village, one hundred and fifty kilometres further on. As I was trying to take a picture of the last passenger struggling to get on, the soldier came and stood sternly right in front of me, saying, "*Nist fotograf!*" (No photograph!). The Persians keep a stern eye on all the reports going out of the country to make sure they only contain ideal images, and as far as possible, nothing unfavourable.

At short intervals along the main roads we came upon the so-called *chai-chanees*, teahouses serving Persia's national drink, tea, and also melons, bread and milk. Everywhere are to be seen the mudwall ruins of old caravanserais which have lost their former importance and fallen into decay. Caravanserais situated at important crossroads have adapted to motor traffic and turned themselves into big garages where you can also get a bed. Sometimes a camel caravan will be resting among the vehicles; ancient and modern peaceably side by side.

Although it is ten times slower to transport things by camel rather than by motor vehicle, it is still cheaper, and it is an interesting fact that petrol is carried to outlying settlements largely by camel caravan. Incidentally, Russian petrol from Baku was more expensive in Northern Persia than in Southern Persia, two thousand kilometres away, where the intention was to undercut the Persian fuel.

It will not be much longer before the motorcar replaces the camel completely. Then the romance of the caravans will only be found in out-of-the way places. But even the car could not entirely deprive the country roads in Persia of their romance. Once we were riding along a bad road in Southern Persia with a bus in front of us. As it was stirring up a great cloud of dust, we preferred to wait until the air was clear again. Suddenly the sound of the engine died away and when the dust had cleared, an extraordinary sight met our eyes. The vehicle had been abandoned in the middle of the road, while the passengers had got out and were kneeling on the hard stony ground, saying their evening prayers. They were all facing in the same direction, westwards towards Mecca. They persisted in this attitude for several minutes as the wind occasionally wafted a few syllables of their monotonous prayers in our direction. When the sun had set and only the bare mountain tops were still glowing red, they stood up, boarded the bus once more and continued their journey, hoping to reach the next caravanserai before dark.

Life on Persian country roads was certainly not lacking in variety. It allowed us many insights into the local way of life. Persians have been used for many generations to travelling the country as nomads. We were always meeting caravans. Some were no more than one or two animals, others were in long trains with bored-looking animals striding along one behind the other. Sometimes it was only one or two camel drivers, at others a whole family group with their chickens and household goods. We usually met up with a caravan when either we or they were taking a rest. The caravans followed an alternative timetable which, to us, especially in the afternoons, seemed more sensible. They would set out at twilight and march in the cool of the night. Daytime was for resting, and the camels, relieved of their burdens, would wander about amidst the sparse grazing. The men slept or rested in the shade of the loads. Thirty or forty kilometres would be covered every night, and whereas we reckoned the length of our journey in days, the caravan people thought in weeks. Often we would take a day's rest with one of these caravans, and took great care not to ride too near the camels, since they had a tendency to panic at the approach of the motorcycle. However, if we kept the bike at a proper distance and did not upset their animals, the caravan people welcomed us most kindly. We were obliged to eat some of their dry bread and drink their lukewarm water. Usually we were only too happy to do so, since we had no bread, and the water in our tanks was nearly boiling hot. Our friends' faces were old, furrowed by wind and sun. They have been travelling for decades, nay, hundreds of years through the deserts of the Middle East, and at their slow and leisurely pace they have covered distances which would go several times round the Earth. We felt rather silly, chuffing urgently away into the distance after only a short stop. Our thirteen thousand kilometres were nothing to these people, eternally on the move.

The people we met were all so different and so friendly, and yet the landscape was so monotonous. The only outstanding feature we came across in the barren desert was a big shining saltmarsh, now completely dried up, it being autumn. In autumn, the surface was as hard, flat and smooth as glass. Wow, that was fun, roaring over the saltmarsh after bumping along the desert tracks! I got a bit reckless and opened up for a short stretch. Soon we were spinning along at sixty, seventy, finally eighty kph! I had quite forgotten how exciting it could be. On the edge of the saltmarsh, in between the sparse tufts of grey 'halva' grass there were even live creatures – thousands of snails living on the dry grasses and getting the moisture they needed from dew at night. It was quite impossible to avoid these fields of snails and a good many of the poor creatures got run over. We became murderers, then mass murderers, and every time it happened we realised how out of place we were here with our machine, disturbing the natural order, and that we had no right to upset the creatures' laborious existence.

The region was completely arid, but around midday we came across a well. It was a cistern roofed over with a construction of stones and mud. The well was deep, maybe nigh on 15 metres. There was neither rope nor windlass. We knotted our straps and tow-ropes together and let down an empty water bottle. There was indeed water in the well, but it was so full of salt that we couldn't drink it. It was a pleasure to be able to wash ourselves, though. We still had enough left to drink in our water tank – some good tea from Badi Massud's kitchen, but think of the hopes and destinies that may have depended on an old well like this in the dreaded Lut desert! It was probably built by Shah Abbas, the mightiest of all Persian rulers, more than three hundred years ago, and must have had many a tale to tell. Our progress through the desert was ten times faster than a camel caravan, and our speed meant that getting water was not really a problem.

We spent the night of 7th to 8th October in the shelter of a deeply eroded *wadi*. Our larder was looking distinctly bare, for we had been so well-fed at Badi Massud's that we had quite forgotten to stock up on provisions. You don't think of food on a full stomach. We made supper off a tin of sardines from our iron rations and for dessert we swallowed a couple of quinine pills, just for luck. Quinine gives you buzzing in the ears, so you can't hear very well, but the stars in the southern sky made the night so magically beautiful that we were yet again perfectly happy in that lonely place. We didn't bother to pitch the tent, but just spread it on the ground and lay down on it, with the power of almighty God above us and the silence of the desert round about us. It was indeed a wonderful life, and how we thanked our stars for the privilege of such a great experience when we were so young. To be sure, there were many things on our journey which we could take in only superficially, but we did so with wholehearted enthusiasm. I do not envy Americans who slave away their entire lives in order to go round the world in their old age. For them, such a journey is the fulfilment of a life, but for us it was an education. It is only today I realise how much we unconsciously learned which can never be learned in school or college.

It is some time since I have said anything about the state of our machine. It was our best friend, of course, and its reliability was often crucial to us. It was no longer shiny and bright as it had been before we left Vienna. No wonder! It had suffered goodness knows how many crashes. The footrests were bent, the wheels were out of true, there was a nasty dent in the tank, and the grips on the handlebars had been stripped off by numerous encounters with the ground.

These were mere details. The main thing was that the engine was still running, and it ran faithfully and without protest for the whole of the long journey. This was nothing short of a miracle. Herbert understood next to nothing of the mysteries of the internal combustion engine, and I was far from being a proper mechanic. Often we never touched a spanner for weeks at a time, unless it was to take off a wheel to mend a tyre. But we never had to do any serious repairs, and that is saying something over thirteen thousand kilometres straight across Asia. We kept the oil and petrol topped up and occasionally de-coked the cylinder head. For everything else we relied on the people who had built the motorcycle, and they didn't let us down.

Tattered and torn and bitten by Persian fleas we rode on south through the Lut desert. The fine strong shoes we had started out with in Vienna had long since given up the ghost. We wore Persian sandals with the advantage that we didn't need to wear socks, these having dissolved completely into holes anyway. Our clothes for travelling through the desert consisted of just a khaki shirt, short trousers and these same Persian sandals. Carefully stowed away in the tent sack we had our 'smart casual' plus-four suits which we intended to don should we receive an invitation from a maharajah in India, rather as a character from a comic strip like Tintin might have done. That was always the way we thought, and that is how it actually happened. The Maharajah Rajah Sabwa Sao Kung Tai Holkar of Indore invited us to his palace in spite of our plus-fours, and we were his guests for a week This made up for all sorts of things that we lacked completely in the desert, but I'll go into that in detail later.

It was still a long way to the wonderland, and even the modest oasis of Hormuk in southern Persia was a goal worth our efforts. There we found fresh tea again and bread. It tasted more wonderful than all the gourmet delights in the world.

Now, from the wide salt desert rose mountains with no way through them. Our road led upwards through a broad stony *wadi* in a fascinating landscape of strangely-shaped mountains glowing in every imaginable colour because of their many different types of rock. It was such odd scenery, the like of which we had never beheld before, that we could almost believe we had been cast away on some planet

Sand dunes in the Lut Desert in southern Persia often come up to the wires of the famous telegraph line. Camera case shows scale. As early as 1861 it was possible to send a telegram from London to Calcutta.

On the edge of the Kavir Desert between Teheran and Meshed virtually no trees grow, hence there is no wood for building houses. Instead of wooden roofs, they build shallow domes from sunbaked mudbricks.

far from Earth. Herbert especially, as a student of geology, was enraptured by the sight and kept yelling, "Stop!" I willingly brought the machine to a halt. Then he would fetch out his little hammer and tap around on the rocks, muttering to himself and giving me a withering glance and shake of the head when I asked him if he'd found gold. Let it not be said that we did no scientific work! My activities consisted mainly in gently persuading Herbert to hand over the stones he had lugged back with him, and throwing them away. With the best will in the world, our light motorcycle was not up to carrying an extra load like that.

Every expedition should really carry some sort of scientific label, but neither Herbert nor I had been able to work up enough enthusiasm for this. Of necessity, we wrote our doctoral theses on Asian problems, but otherwise I don't think we bothered anyone about it. The scientific label makes a certain impression on certain people, but so often one reads in the introduction to a travel book that 'this work is aimed at a wide readership, and the scientific outcomes, which will require more time to evaluate, will be of interest to a different set of readers.' Putting it mildly, this makes me sick. Exceptions by reputable scientists only prove the rule. There are real scientists and there those who just dabble around and they're as different as chalk and cheese. At any rate, Herbert and I were not pretending to do any research. All we wanted was to see whether our strength matched up to our imagination, and to feel the pulse of life in all its forms and colours beating in our veins.

The corrosive salt of the Kavir and Lut deserts was very hard on our machine. The scratches we had got in our crashes healed badly and the *sal-jek* ulcers ate deep into our flesh. We were not in any danger from these as long as we were careful and avoided the risk of blood-poisoning, but they were a nuisance because of the oozing pus. We had sufficient bandages on board, and we did everything possible to keep the wounds clean. Our youthful optimism helped to dispel the very real and justifiable anxiety about blood-poisoning.

# 13
# THE OASIS OF WATER THIEVES

After a journey of several days we at last reached the oasis of Duzdab in Southern Persia. A drearier hole I have seldom seen. At the sight of Duzdab, what springs to mind is the end of the world. Duzdab translates as 'water thief,' and, in former times water was so scarce here and so expensive that people stole it from one another's tents and huts. Today deep wells have been sunk, giving salt water which is rendered drinkable in filtering plants. On closer consideration, Duzdab turns out to be an important place. It lies at the junction of three countries – Persia, Afghanistan and Baluchistan (now part of Pakistan), and is host to a Persian customs post and a branch of the Persian State Bank, albeit at the most basic level. I had seldom been more surprised, and never more glad of meeting a German than there in Duzdab. Herr Schömann was from Stuttgart, and was manager of the Persian bank. Moreover, he was not at all surprised when we turned up at his door.

"You're Reisch and Tichy from Vienna. Welcome, welcome!"

"Did Herr Gold in Teheran tell you we were coming?" we asked, feeling flattered.

"No, but I already knew you'd be coming through Duzdab while you were still on the road somewhere in Asia Minor."

We gave him a puzzled look and he explained. One of the two other Europeans in Duzdab was an Englishman who also worked for a bank. During one of their evening bridge parties (the fourth was a Persian whose standard of play left much to be desired) the Englishman said to Schömann, "I hope your two visitors will play bridge, or one of them, at least."

"What visitors?" asked Schömann.

"The two Viennese students who have just left Istanbul."

The Englishman was not clairvoyant but had a job on the side as a British secret service agent. Somehow we had come to the notice of his colleague in Istanbul and he had signalled news of us to this important border post. Maybe we had been signalled all the way from Vienna to Belgrade and Belgrade to Istanbul, but in the other cities the agents had proved more reticent, probably because they were not looking for someone to make up a four at bridge.

We were a great disappointment in Duzdab since we did not play bridge. Nevertheless, the Englishman probed us in several discreet conversations. Even early on in India we would often be invited by friendly old gentlemen to take a glass of whisky, and then gently quizzed. It was not until after Lahore that these invitations ceased, much to our regret, since it got particularly hot after that and we wouldn't have minded the odd whisky and soda on the rocks. By then they had probably established the fact that we were harmless – rather a slip-up on our part, but you can't think of everything.

Although we were useless as partners at the evening bridge table, Herr Schömann made a great fuss of us. He had volunteered for the post in Duzdab, and, according to his contract, he had to stick it out for four years. When he had signed the contract at the Persian Consulate in Berlin, he had had rather a different picture of the place in mind, but now he was here he was holding out bravely. Herr Schömann was understandably glad of a little variety in his monotonous existence, even if it was only the two ragged Viennese students whom he welcomed enthusiastically to his corrugated-iron bungalow. The first thing he did was to give us permanganate of potash and make us wash our *sal-jek* sores with it. This was a great relief. Then he put up two camp beds for us, dug out a couple of linen sheets from somewhere and put us to bed for five days. Only then did we realise that we actually felt ill. Since Meshed we had not had time to think about it. Looked at from a European point of view, we had become terribly run down and it was high time we got to India where we could expect good roads and every European comfort.

There is not much to tell about Duzdab, the oasis of water thieves. The 'guest room' in Herr Schömann's bungalow was a sort of wash-house in which our camp beds stood. We spent the five days at Herr Schömann's mainly in this room, lying on our beds, for the most part in a very apathetic condition. Now and then we read a bit out of the piles of French magazines in Herr Schömann's possession, but although these magazines were full of stimulating pictures in the best Parisian style, they failed to impress us at all. We were at a very low ebb.

At mealtimes we usually got up and ate with Herr Schömann. The meals were prepared exclusively from tinned food. Where on earth would they have got fresh vegetables in this wretched place that didn't even deserve the name of oasis, and in which I saw not a single palm tree? The main feature of Duzdab was sand, and more sand, with the shifting dunes sometimes reaching as high as the hut roofs. We ran a few experiments while we were there to find the best way of getting through sand dunes. We came to the conclusion that it was much better to pull the machine than to push it. Herr Schömann took photographs of us doing one of these test rides, right in the middle of Duzdab.

Incidentally, Herr Schömann was of the opinion that he would on no account allow us to travel on while we were in such a weakened state. "You must be aware," he reiterated, "that the hardest part of your journey is just beginning. You have probably only the faintest notion of what lies before you. Compared with this, you've had it easy all the way through Syria, Iraq and Persia."

These ominous pronouncements by our host were the best medicine he could have prescribed to raise our spirits. They made us contrary and piqued our sense of sporting honour. The more he warned us, the more we felt our strength returning and the more determined we became to show what we could do. That was more like it!

So it was that, one day, in spite of all his attempts to keep us back, the machine stood ready and waiting for its two riders in the courtyard of Schömann's bungalow. "Good luck, then," said Herr Schömann and took a farewell picture of us with his camera, probably thinking the worst as he did so.

We did experience a few qualms. After all, we were talking about a distance of eight hundred kilometres across sheer sand and stone desert. Was it really so unusual? One year before, I had already covered greater distances in the Sahara desert, and after all, the Syrian desert, the Lut desert in Persia and the Kavir surely counted for something. All these deserts, however, have one great, overriding advantage: they are in part open to motor traffic or they are crossed by busy caravan routes. However lonely it seems, you are never really alone, and in a few days at the most somebody will come by, able to give help, or fetch help, or arrange for help to come. In the Baluchistan desert things were different. Here there was practically no traffic, and we were thrown back on our own resources as never before. If we got stuck here, whether through weakness or a mechanical fault, then we were stuck, full stop.

It would be only by chance, maybe not for many months, that the people at home would learn where the Indian Expedition with the two students had met its end. These were troublesome thoughts, for we loved life, but our ambition proved a stronger influence. Such a shameful end was unthinkable. Death seemed less important to us than the comments which would have passed afterwards. "Those two lads got it into their heads that they could ride a motorcycle to India and now they have both perished miserably. They should never have been allowed to start! What can their parents have been thinking of ... ?" That's the sort of thing the know-alls would be mouthing, in that self-righteous tone, as if they'd always known it would 'end in tears.'

The slightly more reasonable know-alls would say, "At least if they had had two machines, that would have been rather less irresponsible, but to go with just one machine is worse than negligent!"

I can't close my mind to this argument. If each of us had had a motorcycle, then I would have felt easier on that afternoon of 13th October 1933 when we took our leave of Herr Schömann in Duzdab.

"*Auf Wiedersehen!*" we shouted, as the clutch engaged and we wobbled away with our heavily loaded 'pantechnicon' through the courtyard gate.

"*Auf Wiedersehen!*" came the hesitant reply, and Herr Schömann's Persian servants murmured a quiet *inshallah*! ...

# 14

# THE SECOND GREAT CRISIS

We had now embarked on the final and by far the hardest stage of our journey to India. We had already put nine thousand two hundred kilometres behind us since leaving Vienna, and no ordinary kilometres, some of them. They should count double or triple, but that would still be no help in measuring all that our faithful bike had already achieved. Now there were only eight hundred more kilometres left before we would be sailing along the asphalt roads of India. However, these eight hundred kilometres had to be covered through an arid, trackless region with nothing in it but sand and sun, uniting to create a hell on earth. There were some people in Baluchistan, but only way down in the south. In the region that we had to cross there was not even one person per square kilometre, maybe just one per ten square kilometres. We knew that we would now see no humans for a long time, and if by chance one should cross our path, he would fly from us like a startled animal.

The strangest thing about this desert is that it does show traces of human life, and that even Western civilisation once set up shop here. In 1917, when the shadows of the First World War stretched as far as Persia, the British laid a railway from India nearly all the way to the Persian border through the desert. It was a great engineering achievement, opening up communications in a way that only seems possible under the compulsion of war. This railway, built for purely strategic reasons, was useless for peacetime traffic and had long since fallen into disrepair. In some places there was nothing more to be seen of it, since great sand dunes many kilometres wide had covered it. In other places the railway embankment ran across deep *wadis* at almost dizzying heights and now and then one came upon ruined station buildings with enormous water tanks, now rusted through, from which thirsty locomotives once drank. It must have been a busy life on this stretch of the line in those days. Now a pall of silence, desolation and decay had descended.

This railway embankment, which we kept coming across on our journey through Baluchistan, aroused strange and conflicting feelings in us. On the one hand it induced thoughts of civilisation, its protection and safety, whilst on the other we were perfectly aware that this was a delusion. As a result, our solitude and helplessness seemed doubly great and doubly hard to bear. I don't know whether this is the right way to put it, to make it understandable, but it was as if we were travelling from Vienna to Zürich and suddenly there was nothing but desert on the eight hundred kilometres in between. In the place that had been St Pölten, there was nothing but one solitary tamarisk. In Linz we found a Baluchi tomb consisting of a few rocks piled up by human hands in a primitive manner. In Salzburg stood a withered palm tree, and so on, until eventually, after an interminable ride through the desert, we reached our destination, Zürich.

This is rather how the journey through Baluchistan seemed to me, because the railway embankment was a reminder of the throbbing traffic that once upon a time had taken the terror out of the journey – once upon a time, but not very long ago. Now the desert had spread out again and swallowed up the track and its civilised traffic, and here were we, on the most difficult lap of our journey to India.

In 1917 this journey through Baluchistan would have been a mere nothing. We would always have had the railway beside us as a lifeline. If our own strength had failed us, we would have loaded the motorcycle on to a train. In 1933, very little had survived but the memory of this one-time possibility.

Perhaps I am now putting too stark an emphasis on the difficulties, but I have been describing the journey just as it remains in my memory. I still dream sometimes about the feelings I had in Duzdab. It was really just one feeling: fear. I'm not in the least ashamed to admit it. On the journey through Baluchistan so much might have occurred over which we had no control, and that would have been the end. In other areas, even in the most dangerous, there had always been a semblance of authority, order and security – a chief of police or a general. But who had ever heard of a Baluchi chief of police or a Baluchi general? Yet it was not robbers we feared so much as thirst, or rather, dying of thirst.

Even the first few kilometres beyond the oasis of water thieves were quite hard going. The ground was firm enough, but numerous screes and lumps of rock forced us to zigzag constantly, and deep gullies eroded by the water from spring cloudbursts hindered our progress. When would we find the railway embankment Herr Schömann had told us about? On the first day of our Baluchistan journey we covered fifty-six kilometres.

We began to do unpleasant calculations. With this as our daily average, we would need longer than two weeks to get to Quetta. Having said that, our 'road' was for the moment quite a good one, and only rarely did we run into deep sand dunes and have to dig out the machine. Furthermore, we were still full of strength and energy, thanks to Herr Schömann's tinned food. How would it be once we were exhausted? Were we going in the right direction? Would our petrol last out? Would we find water anywhere? Would the machine stand up to it? If not, then what? Why were we doing this? Because we wanted to, because we were young and keen! We had to succeed! That evening, full of thoughts and anxieties like these, isolated in the middle of nowhere, I fell asleep at last.

The new day broke, cloudless as usual. Our limbs were stiff from the chill of the night, and fine dewdrops covered our clothes and the machine.

"You know," I said to Herbert, "we'll be thinking about this journey for the rest of our lives, and the older we get, the more we'll think about it."

"Quite right. Distance lends enchantment to the view. Later on, our toughest moments of physical and emotional strain will seem like the height of happiness." Herbert was such a romantic.

"Actually I was thinking of something else – the older we get, the more we'll suffer from rheumatism."

Herbert laughed. "You're a bit previous with all this worry! The first thing is to do our damnedest to get out of this hell of sand and sun. You just concentrate on keeping the machine in one piece."

Herbert's misgivings were only too right. We set about our morning's work in silence, frozen to the marrow in our damp clothes. Herbert packed up the sleeping bags and stowed them on the machine. The air mattresses' days were over – the ants had eaten right through them. They wouldn't keep the air in any more and every few hours we would wake up because a sharp stone would be sticking into us through the empty mattress. In the end we threw them away and slept on the hard ground. At least you knew then what you were dealing with.

While Herbert was collecting up our pitiful household belongings from the desert and strapping them on to every conceivable part of the bike, I occupied myself with the engine. Just lately, our good old friend had been very reluctant to start. The electric cables were cracking because of the great changes in temperature and the effects of salt in the Kavir desert. The ignition current was flashing around everywhere and just not getting to the plug.

If it had been possible to push-start the machine, things would have been easier, but I would defy anyone to push our 'pantechnicon,' weighing over two hundred kilograms, through sand and scree. It would have tried the strongest physique.

We just had to wait. By dint of patience and the sun's rays, we dried out and so did the cables. Our spirits rose, in spite of our empty stomachs, when blue smoke puffed merrily from the exhaust pipe. A new day for the expedition had begun. It was the ninety-fourth day of our journey to India.

The heat of the sun soon became unbearable. It fell on us from above, hostile and fiery, and bounced back off stone and sand with added force. The usual form of mirage, which we had already seen many times before, played before us. The bare hills nearby and the Afghan mountains in the distance seemed to be hovering in mid-air, cut off from the ground. It looked as if theatre scenery had been let down from the flies and not quite reached the stage. In between these hovering mountains and the ground, water was visible. It was so clear and so blue that one could not imagine a more enticing spectacle for a wanderer in the desert. This apparent water was nothing but the reflection of the sky, caused by alternate layers of air of different heat and permeability. The Arabs call this natural phenomenon *Bacher el Alfrid* – the water of the Devil, and it is true that with this water the Devil has lured many a son of the desert down to hell.

The mirage of popular imagination – the illusion of oases, towns, groups of palm trees – is much rarer. For this, it is necessary to have several reflections functioning at the same time in order to produce the image, which may be either the right way or the wrong way up. In actual fact, you will only get this mirage when there really is an oasis, town or group of palm trees at a distance of between fifty and a hundred kilometres. The big question is 'where?' There is usually not much point in going straight in the direction of the image, since the effect of refraction can also work very strongly sideways. In addition, the image is constantly shifting about with fluctuations in the layers of air.

Thus one should never rely on a mirage, but rather on good maps, the compass and the odometer, although one often comes near to losing faith in these aids, and nothing is more fatal or more dispiriting than the feeling of travelling into a void.

In the end we did find the railway embankment. *Al-hamdu Allah!* Thanks and praise be to Allah, Lord of the deserts. This railway embankment was the ultimate signpost for us. It was bound to get us to India. We felt a considerable sense of relief in having this strip of human civilisation running alongside us. The embankment was high and it was a muscular *tour de force* to hoist our fully-loaded machine to the top of it. It was a bumpy ride going over one sleeper after another but vastly preferable to the nasty pits in the desert sand.

Unfortunately, this ideal rail trip did not last long. A high sand dune had drifted over the embankment. I took a run at it and both of us flew in an elegant arc down the sand hill. Another crash – we had lost count by now. At the beginning of the journey, Herbert had attempted to keep count but gave up – I think it was at number one hundred and seventeen.

In spite of all this practice at crashing, I ended up lying underneath the machine. The 'pantechnicon' lay on top of me like heavy rock, with the exhaust pipe burning into my thigh in no uncertain fashion. Herbert freed me from my fiery burden and we both silently resumed our struggle along the treacherous railway. The hard knocking against the sleepers offended my technical sensibilities – would everything be all right? Even our efficient Puch wouldn't stand this for any length of time. I searched my mind for a remedy. Alongside the sleepers ran a footpath, thirty centimetres wide, on which I thought it should be possible to ride. It would have been perfectly all right if the embankment had not been three to four metres high. Plunging off that would be extremely unpleasant and would far exceed the acceptable risks of a normal crash in the desert. We tried it all the same. This balancing act made me go hot and cold, since it had a nasty little danger of its own: the narrow strip of path had a hardened crust on it from the winter rains – rather like the frozen crust we get on snow. If I drove slowly, we broke through the crust into soft sand, so the situation compelled me to go along the track-edge at speed. My heart was soon pounding. After all, I wasn't trained for the circus!

We were lucky and covered quite a distance in this manner, but I was glad when the crazy ride came to an end where the embankment had been washed away and the rails were left hanging in mid-air.

After this we met with similar interruptions more and more frequently, and eventually gave up using the railway. However, it showed us the way. Late in the afternoon we saw a building in the distance. It took us two more hours to make our way to it. This was not always easy, since we had left our spades behind somewhere, and shovelling sand with our hands was a laborious business. I removed the Persian number plate which we had acquired in Teheran and used it as a shovel. Herbert once took a photograph of me doing this. Taking pictures was always a drag, because when the going was really tough, we had other things on our mind. Today, however, I'm very glad that we occasionally made that extra effort to get it done.

The building on the side of the railway embankment seemed to me just right for an overnight stay. It was a cheerful prospect after our previous damp bivouac on the bare earth.

In 1917, during the First World War, the British drove a railway through Baluchistan from India to Persia. In 1933 this strategic line lay in ruins. It provided a sort of a signpost for us, but wasn't any real help – rather the opposite.

We made plenty of noise with our machine running in first gear, but no living creature showed itself. Before us stood the remains of a railway station, it was a massive building, reminiscent of a fortified caravanserai, ringed by a rampart about four metres high, and with only a single gate on the side next the track. This was of steel, badly rusted. We tried the heavy handle in vain. It was stuck and showed signs of unsuccessful forcing.

Feeling that it would still be interesting to get inside this fortress-like station, we walked round the outer walls and found that nature had provided us with the best possible means of entry. On one side, a sand dune had drifted up against the high wall, and we climbed it without difficulty. Now we could see down into the courtyard, which seemed to lie under a spell of desolation.

The station premises were built against the high outer wall at ground level. Doors and windows had gone. Nomads had probably carried them off as valuable fuel for their fires. Deep sand lay everywhere, and with a couple of jumps we were down in the courtyard. We passed our sleeping things, food and cooker in through the bars of one of the outside windows, leaving the bike standing in the open.

In the middle of the yard was a cistern, filled to the brim with drifting sand, but we had plenty of water and tea, having learned to get by on very little liquid. We sat down on the edge of the cistern to prepare supper. We had eaten nothing till then except a few dates.

Stuck in the sand – an everyday occurrence. The motorcycle is being laboriously dug out. Physically, we were frequently close to exhaustion and mentally close to despair. A motorcycle had never before been through the hell of Baluchistan. No motorcycle had yet got to India by land. Would we make it?

"I'm starving," I said to Herbert, "Isn't it time we opened The Tin?"

This Tin had become legendary to us. We had acquired it in the Meshed bazaar. The venerable shopkeeper had called it 'American meat', but the label had long since departed and the thing was full of dents and rather rusty. We had already lugged this tin for more than a thousand kilometres and had frequently resisted the temptation to open it and devour the delicious meat.

"I think so," agreed Herbert.

Today we should have a festive menu, firstly because we were spending the night in an 'hotel,' secondly because we were ravenous, and thirdly because the tin was so heavy and every kilo had to be saved if possible.

I set about the task ceremoniously.

"What do you think is in there, Herbert?"

"Ham," said Herbert.

But it was stewed rhubarb, which was the last thing we would have expected. We cursed that scoundrel in the Meshed bazaar in the Oriental manner with fulsome and frightful curses. In the end, we resigned ourselves to the old proverb that 'Persia is where lies have the longest legs.' All the same, legs over a thousand kilometres long were really a bit much. Supper, therefore, consisted of the usual flatbread, the usual dates out of our bag, and – you've guessed – stewed rhubarb. Another of our illusions had been shattered.

We set up camp in one of the rooms. There was sand here too, up to our ankles,

| Riding on the abandoned railway lines in the Lut desert.

but we were thankful for it. It was soft and dry, besides which it formed a protective blanket over all the old tin cans, rusty bits of machinery, broken equipment and other remains of a vanished civilisation.

Through the empty door-opening, I could look out from where I lay at the sand-filled cistern in the yard. In times gone by, it must have been lovely to be able to draw up water by the bucketful and have a really good wash.

It seemed to me as if shadows and white figures were flitting noiselessly about within the deserted walls, but it was probably only my overwrought nerves, making me see ghosts. I willed myself to sleep.

A surprise awaited us next morning. Where was our stack of bread? Where was our bag of dates? We had left our provisions on the edge of the cistern, we were quite sure we had, but how ever hard we looked, they were not to be found. However, we could see prints of bare feet in the sand. Were there people here after all? A Baluchi must have watched us as we came along and secretly followed us. Now we had lost over half our food. That was bad.

"A good thing we ate up The Tin yesterday," said Herbert in an attempt at sarcasm.

Whether the nocturnal visitor would have taken the tin with him is another question. The fellow had not gone for the machine: probably he had been afraid to touch it. A strange thing like that must be the work of the Devil.

We rode for five days though the wastes of Baluchistan that are shunned by God and man alike. Then we came upon people, nomads who had put up a few tents near the tomb of a saint. Their goats stank at ten metres, with the wind the other way, but we greedily gulped down great draughts of their milk. The people gave us bread too, in the shape of a flat cake three quarters of a metre in length that looked for all the world like an old towel. The tents were filled with all the odours of the Orient except, that is, for the ones extolled in fairytales. We took great care when breathing in and were thankful for the shade. In recognition of the hospitality we had enjoyed, we presented the people with a propelling pencil. There was great happiness all round. I believe these people are more contented than we are. To need little is to be always rich.

An old man sat near the tomb of the saint, toiling honestly to form a pot from clay with his bare hands. In view of the nearby tomb, I could not help thinking of the words of the Persian poet, Omar Khayyám:

*For I remember stopping by the way*
*To watch a Potter thumping his wet Clay:*
*And with its all-obliterated tongue*
*It murmur'd – "Gently, Brother, gently, pray!"*

These were the first people we had seen for many days and they had been kind to us. Maybe it was because they were so incredibly poor that they had shared with us everything they possessed. We asked how far it was to Quetta.

Quetta? They had never heard the name before. Their world was the desert and Quetta lay in faraway India. Going by our maps and the distance we had covered so far, we estimated about another four hundred kilometres. That was going to be another hard slog, and the motorcycle was giving me plenty of cause for anxiety. Because of our wild ride along the railway track and the constant bumping over stony ground, spokes in the back wheel had been snapping, one after the other with remorseless regularity. Every morning I had a tricky time fixing the remaining spokes so that they were spread evenly around the rim, until my fingers were scratched and bloody, but it was no good. The back wheel was no longer round, but was becoming more and more of an oval. Eventually, I took nine spokes out of the front wheel and fixed them in the back. That was all right for another half a day, but what would we have given for a few dozen spokes! We would have exchanged everything we had on board, valued at several thousand *Schilling*, for a handful of spokes costing one or two *Schilling*, if only we had been able to buy them. But any shop selling spares was too far away to be reached.

We did not talk much during this time. Death was breathing down our necks, for, if the back wheel collapsed, we would be done for – finally done for. Herbert dragged himself for long distances on foot in order to take the weight off the machine. I drove as carefully as if I had had enormous eggshells on the axles instead of wheels, but it was all no good. The wheels went on getting squarer, and we waited from one hour to the next for the final collapse.

We were sure that in India we would be able to get spokes of some sort which could be filed down to fit, but Nushki, the nearest town, was still hundreds of kilometres away. Neither of us would have managed this distance on foot, as we were nothing but skin and bone, and as for the strong will with which we had set out so gaily and so full of courage in search of wonders, all that time ago − it had been failing for some time now.

There was still a light in our eyes, but it was no longer the light of confidence, more a feverish flame that often flickered dangerously when our glances met.

We were thirsty, and had only one goatskin of water left. The flies maddened us and drove us half crazy. Where did these pests come from in the middle of the desert? To begin with, we were completely mystified, and then we discovered that they were travelling with us on parts of the machine sheltered from the wind. These were flies from the nomad camp by the saint's tomb. We were also plagued with vast numbers of fleas in our luggage, so at night we were bitten to the bone, and by day, whenever we stopped to rest or to mend something, we were attacked by flies. They flew into our mouths when we were eating because it was moist and shady in there. When we spat them out they seemed almost offended.

I laboured under a silent reproach for not having brought enough spokes. Herbert never said anything, but he was right. What use were the heavy axles and springs, pistons and bearings, cogwheels and couplings? What use was the spare magneto, the complete carburettor, when our fate hung on a couple of spokes? It was enough to drive one mad. I believe that Herbert hated me then. People on other expeditions have murdered one another in similar situations. They have even eaten one another when driven by hunger.

We had lugged thirty kilos of spare parts for more than ten thousand kilometres halfway across Asia, and for nothing! Now we made up our minds to ditch the lot. There they lay in the desert, all those expensive spare parts, but still we had no spokes.

We grew fatalistic and let ourselves believe that our machine would achieve the impossible. Both wheels together had long since been running on fewer spokes than we would have considered the minimum for *one* wheel on a good road, and yet we were still going. Thus it seemed probable that we would still be riding on half the present number of viable spokes, in fact, why not with no spokes at all? We were ready to believe in miracles, and soon came the first reward for our belief.

The narrow valley bordered by two high dunes widened out somewhat and suddenly there was a plain ahead of us, as smooth as a mirror, shimmering white. It was a dried out salt lake. In summer its surface consisted of a layer of mud dried as hard as stone, offering a surface far superior to the best asphalt in the world.

After days of struggling on through the deep sand of the burning dunes, metre by metre, we now sped at sixty kph across the hard mud. The shores disappeared in the flickering air, and in the middle of the lake stood a solitary camel. It stared in amazement at the motorcycle roaring towards it and turned to flee. Unfortunately we soon came to the end of the lake and had to cross another belt of dunes. We had still seen no sign of a human being in all this desolation, and we looked for the way east to India by our compass. The sun blazed down on us with colossal strength, but for many kilometres there was no shade save that of our little machine, in which we rested from time to time.

No sound was to be heard in the vast wilderness, no movement to be seen, only the burning air flickering over the dead landscape where nothing grew. Suddenly a Baluchi appeared from behind a sand hill and came slowly towards us. In his hand he held an ancient rifle. His dark brown face stood out strangely against his snow-white linen clothing. This man had very likely seen only a few Europeans in his life, and certainly no motorcycle. Nevertheless, his proud, dismissive gaze rested on us for only a moment. Then he passed us without a greeting and disappeared behind the sand dunes without turning round.

A strange, proud people!

After a short rest we went on again. To one side ahead of us a huge cube was hovering in the air, one of the numerous mirages. We were unable to tell whether it was a small block of stone a few metres away or a mountain lying many kilometres further off. More beautiful than this apparition were the innumerable lakes which we constantly saw ahead of us. I have never in my life seen such fantastically beautiful landscapes with lakes as we did in waterless Baluchistan. Green trees and palms surrounded the still blue waters in which jagged mountains were reflected. Sometimes we even thought we could see little boats floating on the surface of the water. It was most peculiar. Long experience had taught us that these lovely lakes were only delusions brought on by the excessive strain on our nerves, through harsh sunlight and heat. When we came nearer they would dissolve into sand. All the same, we repeatedly experienced the vague hope that it might really be a lake where we could drink and escape from the atrocious heat for a short time by bathing in its waters.

Luck was with us. After a short time we met nomads from whom we received water and Asian flatbread. There was a small Baluchi village ahead of us. At the noise of the engine, the men came out of the huts but the women were shy and hid, taking timid glances from under their red headscarves at the two foreigners. Soon we were sitting in a circle with the men, eating wonderful warm bread, which only smelt slightly of mutton fat, and eagerly drinking muddy, foul-tasting water.

One of our hosts brought out a dish made of rice, onions and garlic. In spite of hunger and goodwill, we were quite unable to eat any of the peppery food. We handed it back to our benefactor with thanks, but instead of accepting it, he threw it to the dogs with a great gesture. Anything touched by a Christian, an unclean person, may no longer be eaten by the faithful. When we came to go, we tried to give our hosts money, but they refused it proudly, saying that it was their duty, which they took for granted, to feed us. On no account would they take money.

*"Salem aleikum"* – peace be with you, they said as we left, and we replied courteously *"Aleikum salem"* – with you be peace. And there really was a great peace and an atmosphere of happiness lying over this poverty-stricken village.

As we travelled on, we began to come upon occasional tamarisks, and once or twice we saw half-obliterated vehicle tracks in the sand, probably made by British gazelle hunters from Quetta. We knew now that the most difficult part was already behind us. This came not a moment too soon, for our physical condition – to say nothing of the state of the wheels on our machine – was now most pitiful, and our sex appeal, if indeed we had ever had any, had sunk to zero. Our faces, burnt black by the sun, were covered with stubbly beard, the skin of our lips was roughened and split, and our eyes were red and inflamed. We had long since run out of sunblock but were getting quite good results with, guess what, engine oil. Less successful was the time in Persia when we used engine oil to fry four eggs. The taste was perfectly acceptable, but the after-effects were calamitous. Every few kilometres I had to stop the motorcycle because one or other of us had to disappear in a hurry.

In the evening we reached another nomad encampment. We were now sure that we would reach our destination and would be arriving in Nushki, a small town on the Indian-Baluchistan border, the following day.

Around the black Bedouin tent a few cows and sheep were grazing and a picturesquely-dressed woman was busy milking the animals. A little crippled Baluchi boy inquisitively fingered our clothes while we conversed with his white-bearded father. Meanwhile, the sun had gone down and the mountains cast purple shadows into the broad valley. Suddenly, the crippled gnome pulled himself up – until now we had claimed his entire attention – and dragged himself a little way out into the steppe. There he knelt down, with his unlovely twisted face transfigured, looking westwards toward Mecca. He bowed his poor body in prayer and his lips whispered fervent words. Although still so ugly, his face now seemed almost beautiful.

The dusk deepened, it grew cool, and we crawled into our tent feeling somehow less than glad that Baluchistan, the hardest part of our journey, was now behind us.

The first signs of roadbuilding now began to appear and then there was actually a bridge spanning one of the deeply carved, dry stream beds in a bold arc. To the objective viewer it was probably only a poor wretched little bridge, but when was the last time we had seen a bridge? And how many hours of heavy labour, often in the worst of the summer heat, had it cost to construct an effective causeway across the crumbling ravines of the countless *wadis*? There was no bridge in the world to compare with the one at Nushki.

No European lived in Nushki. The Indian mayor invited us to his house and fed us sumptuously. How marvellously cool it was under his roof.

Late in the afternoon we travelled on. The road was now clearly marked. It was not exactly a road, but rather two wheel tracks in the dry level surface of the desert, smooth and easy, with no stones or sand.

Up until nightfall we were much occupied in trying to outwit a young camel. It was standing on the track ahead of us, and I drove slowly up to it. We thought that it would behave like any reasonable camel and either take a couple of steps sideways to let us go by or stay standing on the track and force us to make a detour. We would have been perfectly sympathetic, this being camel country, not motorcycle country, but the camel did neither. It ran away from us along the track. On a good road this behaviour would not have been so absurd, but it seemed to be mesmerised by the two narrow wheel tracks like a rabbit caught in the headlights! We attempted to make a wide detour around the camel, but the ground off the track was covered with stones and we only made very slow progress. Meanwhile the camel ran at a leisurely pace along the smooth road, keeping the same distance ahead of us. This overtaking strategy failed several times. We were absolutely infuriated with the camel for obliging us to ride rough, when we had a proper road again after so long, so we tried what speed could do. When that camel feels us tickling his backside, we thought, he'll soon think better of it and move over. We drove at forty, then at forty-five kph, and the camel charged along ahead of us. We could go no faster on our

An old Baluchi shows particular interest in this thin rubber raincoat. The young people keep a respectful distance from the strange vehicle.

bent wheels, so we tried to forget our sympathy for the camel and to take no notice of its dancing about all over the road like a mirage. It must have been very tired by now. It looked so sweet and lovable whenever it turned round to look at us, as if pleading for help. Suddenly, for no apparent reason, the camel stepped sideways and allowed us to pass. The last time we saw it, it was trotting slowly back again along the track.

Are there still miracles? A few, surely. The strange wide ribbon ahead of us, winding through the valley, was a tarmac road. We stopped, got off the machine and felt the smooth road surface with our hands. We felt like kissing it.

*VISIT VELOCE ON THE WEB – WWW.VELOCE.CO.UK*
*All current books • New book news • Special offers • Gift vouchers • Forum*

*133*

# 15
## LATIF HAMID AND THE DYNAMO

It was just a few more kilometres to Quetta (in India then, but now in modern day Pakistan), and already the outline of the city was visible ahead, a real city such as we had not seen since Teheran.

We wanted our arrival to be as decent as we could make it, so we called a short halt in a caravanserai and attempted to wash and shave at its well. I use the word 'attempted' advisedly, since we were not very successful. I don't know whether it was our somewhat unrefined odour after nearly a week of desert travel, or the heady perfume of our shaving cream, or perhaps the startling combination of both which suddenly attracted a vast swarm of monstrous wasps. They were as big as hornets and were determined to get a taste of the shaving cream. Since we had already got this on to our faces, we were pretty alarmed. Herbert got stung first, then I was, and then Herbert again. After that, we fled. Fled is the word – we left our shaving brushes behind, noticing with amazement that the wasps of Quetta were capable of attaining a speed of 40kph. Having a good clear road, we soon shook off the last of our pursuers. Herbert, on the pillion, had to fight the rearguard action and was stung again in the process, and in the one place that had not been soaped. He complained bitterly and said he would rather do the remaining kilometres on foot than stay sitting down a minute longer. But we had already arrived.

Latif Hamid, an Indian businessman whom we had met in the course of our studies in Vienna, gave us a warm welcome. He got us into a bath and gave us new clothes. The next morning, just as we were stretching ourselves luxuriously one more time in our soft beds, an incredible, incomprehensible sound reached our ears. As a special surprise for us, Hamid had turned on the wireless and we heard quite clearly, with almost no interference, "This is Radio Vienna ending our broadcast for today. The time is 23.30. *Gute Nacht!*"

So we were actually in India (today Pakistan). Whatever happened now, we had reached our destination, no matter that it was only, technically speaking, the most westerly administrative tip of that enormous empire. We reminded ourselves what we had expected of India, and what our friends in Vienna had expected of our Indian experiences, especially the linguists who knew how to say 'I love you' in Czech, Hungarian, and of course in Italian. For them we were charged with bringing back this declaration of affection in as many Indian dialects and languages

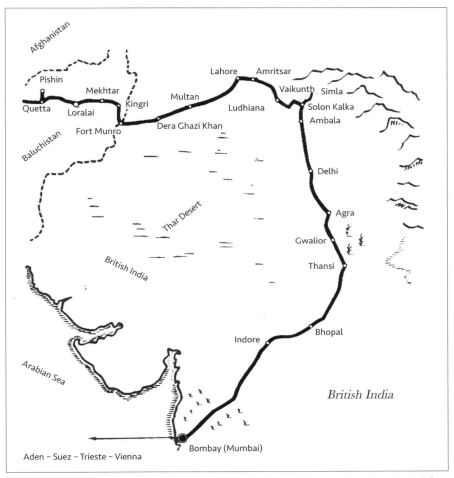

Map of the route through Baluchistan and British India (now Pakistan and modern-day India).

as possible for their collection, but the first Indian words we learned were *Garam pani lao* and *Tanta pani lao*, meaning 'Bring hot water' and 'Bring cold water.' This pathetic request bore no relation to the linguistic demands made on us, but was our constant form of address to Latif Hamid's Indian servant when requesting that he provide suitable quantities of hot and cold water for treating our *sal-jek* ulcers. It was Latif's own theory that the sores would respond to frequent immersion at alternating extreme temperatures over many hours. We did a lot of this, therefore, sitting all the while in Latif's cool guest room and feeling very fortunate.

After a week we had made such good progress, both physically and mentally, that we were ready to continue our journey. Latif Hamid agreed, saying helpfully, "I'll go and see whether your dynamo is ready." Our dynamo unit had been in need of a thorough overhaul, and Latif had made himself responsible for taking it to an electrical engineer.

"It won't be ready until tomorrow," he said, so we went on with the hot and cold bathing for another day. The following day, the answer was again "Tomorrow", and this went on for some time. Then I discovered the dynamo lying on top of Latif's cupboard.

"But it's here on your cupboard!" I said.

"Yes," he replied, "It's been there for a week. It's been ready all this time, but I couldn't bear to lose your company!"

Now he had no choice. We just had time to write one more hasty love letter for him to one of his girlfriends in Vienna – he maintained a protracted correspondence with a large section of the female Viennese population on the strength of a German vocabulary not much larger than our Persian one. Then we said farewell to Latif and his family. In fact, this meant only the male family members, for, as a pious Moslem, he kept the women away in a separate part of the house, into which we were never allowed a look. Although he recounted quite a lot of details of his private life in Vienna, we never managed to find out how many wives he had to his name here at home. Apparently, there was a wide gulf between the 'Mitzis' of Vienna, whose charms and idiosyncrasies provided the talking point for many a delightful evening, and the 'Zuleikas' of Quetta who were kept scrupulously hidden from strangers, and very likely from other friends, too. In the evenings, therefore, we were the centre of attention for a great gathering of menfolk – brothers, cousins, uncles, nephews or simply acquaintances of Mr Latif, but the female equivalents – sisters, cousins, aunts, nieces, and friends – did not come. Maybe they did come, however, and simply remained in that part of the house where we supposed Mr Latif's wives to be, the part to which we had always been denied access. This part of the house offered its occupants unexpected opportunities for their own amusement. It was separated from our apartments by a courtyard and stood a little higher. Its windows were hung with heavy curtains which made it impossible to see into the interior, while allowing the occupants a clear view to the outside. We often noticed a tell-tale movement of the curtains, as if an over-inquisitive nose were pressed against them or as if people were jostling for position. There were scenes enough in our rooms to set off such jostling. For instance, we would be sitting there opposite them in the midday sun, stark naked with only a towel round our loins, grimacing with agony as we dipped our *sal-jek* sores first in cold water and then in hot. This alone must have presented a most entertaining spectacle. In addition, Herbert had that wasp sting in a place no wasp should really have been able to get at if he had only been sitting tight in the saddle instead of standing up and laying about him like a knight in battle, the better to beat the creatures off. This last wasp sting was showing signs of turning into a *sal-jek*, so Herbert performed the most extraordinary gymnastics in order to give this part of his body hot and cold dips too. I am quite sure we did not disappoint Mr Latif's ladies. Perhaps it was because of their pleadings that he kept back our dynamo for so long.

All the same, by 24th November 1933 we had reinstalled the dynamo and were ready to proceed. We had even managed to get hold of some spokes from a motorised Gurkha regiment, and the faithful Puch, rejuvenated, could now be let loose on India's roads.

Latif Hamid in Quetta nursed us back to health and proved himself a true friend by the many services he did us. We set off again for India, refreshed and strengthened. Latif Hamid is on the left beside the motorcycle.

Thank you, dear Latif, for the many happy hours we spent at your house. In that time we made so many plans. Latif wanted to come to Vienna again, and we were going to pay him another visit in Quetta. We were brimming over with ideas. Latif never came to Vienna again, but two years later I came to Quetta in a car. A few days previously, one of the biggest earthquakes of the century had devastated western India, and Baluchistan in particular. Little remained of that fine city. Since then we have become accustomed to such sights, but it was new to me then and it shook me deeply. I almost failed to find the street where we had lived. There were smoking ruins and people weeping as they searched for survivors. In the place where Latif's house had stood there were likewise only ruins. Some people who were digging there told me that Latif and his family had perished.

We were ignorant of all this as we departed, and it was a joyful farewell, full of the expectation of meeting again in Vienna or Quetta. Then we rode out along Quetta's huge wide tarmac streets into the suburbs, and left the big city behind.

One can't help wondering how such a large modern city could spring up in this poverty-stricken country, for the land here is still desert – no longer the deadly and completely sterile desert of western Baluchistan, but desert nonetheless, with little means of supporting life. The answer is that Quetta is on the one hand an oasis, and also a trading post, like Kandahar to the north and Herat to the northwest. It is a town traversed by ancient caravan routes, the frontier fort of various geographical and racial areas, a place where goods are exchanged, an oasis with water and its own agriculture. These are the age-old reasons for Quetta's existence. The new reasons, which led to the creation of a large modern city, were Britain's anxieties about India. Throughout almost the whole period of British rule in India, the menacing shadow of the Russian bear in the north lay on the British sahibs like an incubus. Of course, in the north the impenetrable barrier of the Himalaya gave protection, but towards Afghanistan, the frontier lay open, and the bear from the north had a gateway through which to invade. It was better not to go as far as Kabul to take on the bear. This had been tried twice and each time had resulted in a bloody rebuff, thanks to the Afghans. After this, suitable sites around Afghanistan had been fortified and turned into garrison towns.

Peshawar, Kohat, Bannu, Quetta, which in themselves were only little oases and caravan towns, became centres of activity in the worldwide British Empire. At a time when Kipling still sang of India in immortal verses, and when the new age of equality had yet to begin in London, then whisky and money flowed freely, even in the farthest outposts of British power. A host of underlings was necessary for the conversion of money into goods and fighting strength. British Tommies, Gurkhas from Nepal, various Indian auxiliary troops were all rich folk in the poor desert region. They liked spending money, and in this way mighty cities grew up in the otherwise impoverished frontier regions. One of these was Quetta.

We rode north towards Kandahar. The name of this Afghan city must be familiar to every skier from the name of the Kandahar Race, but he is unlikely to make any connection with the city. Neither did I at the time, or if I did, I was going the wrong way. I was surprised that a Tyrolean or Swiss word should have become the name of an Afghan city. Of course, it was the other way round. A British general (whose name I have forgotten), fought a decisive battle in the region of Kandahar, and was thereupon elevated to the title of Earl of Kandahar. It was he who donated the challenge trophy for the ski race.

About halfway to the Afghan border we made a halt in Pishin. A relative of the Afghan King Amanullah, a venerable Afghan by the name of Sadar Joffer Khan (his relationship by marriage to the king earned him respect, even though the latter had been deposed) had extended an invitation to us. The Birjand performance was now repeated on a more lavish scale. Two cars came out to meet us on the road and escorted us back in triumph. The population made a guard of honour, the Khan greeted us in the manner of an Oriental monarch. His cousin, however, who was a real Oriental monarch, had got it into his head to become a sort of Western-style reformer and president. This had not appealed to the Afghans, and they had driven him out. He had gone to Rome, but Sadar Joffer Khan was waiting only a few kilometres outside Afghanistan for things to sort themselves out inside the country. The Afghans were a restless people who laid great store by their tribal independence. Anything might happen, and the first one to arrive in Kabul or Kandahar had a good chance of becoming the country's ruler. It was possible that Sadar Joffer was only staying in Pishin because he had large estates there and liked the country life. He talked enthusiastically and at length about his country, compared with which Persia was nothing but a dreary desert which had formerly been a province of Afghanistan, and India was a burning-hot jungle, likewise a former province of Afghanistan. We were often amused by his patriotism.

Helmut Hahmann with our Steyr-100 expedition car in the ruins of Quetta.

But the old Khan was not so wrong after all. Later on, I travelled widely in Afghanistan, and Herbert also spent a long time in that country. We both felt very much at ease there and were truly sorry to leave it, I to travel on to the 'province' of India and Herbert to the 'province' of Persia. After Afghanistan, I found India too hot and too civilised. Herbert found Persia too tame and too modern.

Our stay with Sadar Joffer had only one disadvantage in that it followed directly on the hospitality of Latif. Had we arrived straight from the desert at the Khan's house, then the ice-cold drinks, the roast mutton, gazelle and chicken would probably have kept us there for weeks. As it was, it was merely a heightened pleasure from which we were able to detach ourselves after a few days.

This account may give rise to the impression that we were particularly addicted to culinary and alcoholic delights. This is untrue. We ate and drank with as much pleasure as any healthy young people, only in the course of the trip we developed a kind of hunger psychosis. This is the personal experience of anyone who has eaten little and irregularly over a long period. Peter Fleming, who undertook a daring journey from Peking to India, gives an excellent description of it in his book *News from Tartary*. His little caravan was making its way through a majestic valley, with colossal mountain ranges on either side, and stunning views into the distance, but what was his constant preoccupation and what did he spend hours discussing with the woman who accompanied him? The evening meal! Would he manage to shoot a hare? Would they roast it or stew it in gravy? A few noodles would go nicely with the gravy. And so it went on for hours as they traversed a truly breathtaking landscape.

Maybe it was only the noise of the engine, making any conversation difficult, which prevented similar confessions. At least we can truthfully say that we did not actually talk about food that often.

*VISIT VELOCE ON THE WEB – WWW.VELOCE.CO.UK*
*All current books • New book news • Special offers • Gift vouchers • Forum*

*140*

# 16
# THE MAP OF INDIA

We were now riding through an area of great beauty, where high mountains, isolated patches of green vegetation and numerous mountain streams were interspersed with forlorn desert country. The resulting mixture was both beautiful and impressive. It was here that we came across a place called Loralai (*sic*). Herbert had a go at the famous song, with *"Ich weiß nicht, was soll es bedeuten ... ,"* but, as he can't sing, I was obliged to speed up so that the airstream would carry his song away from my ears. The mountains of the Sulaiman range still lay ahead of us, and then came the Indian plain. I headed straight for it.

The area had military significance, and as war fathers all things, it also fathers good roads, so it was on a good road that we kept riding far into the night. We were dead tired when we lay down at the roadside on a piece of flat ground and fell asleep immediately.

I must have been sleeping so deeply that I did not turn over very much, otherwise I would not be telling this story. I was awakened by Herbert grabbing my arm and hauling me vigorously towards him. His behaviour was enough to scare me, although I was still drunk with sleep. Could he have gone crazy? Anxiety was written all over his face and he kept holding me tight up against him, staring rigidly past me. Oh, I thought, a scorpion, he's seen a scorpion! Then I turned round too and looked where Herbert was looking. I saw immediately why I had thought for a moment that Herbert had gone crazy. He had that strange distant expression often seen on mad people of the quiet and dreamy sort. However, he was not mad: he really *was* looking into the distance. Two or three feet from where I had been sleeping, the mountain fell away vertically for several hundred metres, and below us lay the Indian plain spread out like a map. With great caution we packed up our sleeping gear and tiptoed softly back to the safety of the roadway.

The lavish meat diet provided by Latif and Sandar Joffer had spoiled us. We were hungry, although we still had stores of bread and fruit, more than we had often had to eat in a week in the past. In a little rivulet flowing across the road we saw a strange creature. It looked something like a fat snake or eel or a very long fish with shrunken fins. Neither of us had enough training in natural history to enable us to identify the species, nor were we sufficiently interested. We slew the creature by throwing a couple of well-aimed stones at it, skinned it, and roasted it over a wood fire. It tasted excellent. This was the only successful hunting feat of our entire trip. Later on, with the Maharajah of Indore, we tried our luck with gazelles, but they were much nippier than our fish-snake and we were having to shoot with rifles. Although the court gamekeeper drove the gazelles right under our noses, something previously unheard-of in the state's hunting annals came to pass: guests of the Maharajah returned home with an empty bag! We lost much face, and the gamekeeper may have lost his job.

The burning heat of India enveloped us. We were in Sind province, a poor, desert-like region in the north of the Thar Desert. In many respects it reminded us of the dry areas we had already come through, except that the vegetation, where there was any, was actually tropical, an impenetrable mass of greenery with palm-trees, creepers and gaudy blossoms. The first little monkeys gave us mocking stares.

Where the sand became too deep, wire netting had been laid over the surface and this prevented us from sinking in. This is a cheap and simple way of providing a solid roadsurface even in the shifting ground of a desert. It had only one drawback: individual links would sometimes stick up like snares, and odd parts of the motorcycle would get caught in them. Then we would suddenly be brought up short, but as soon as we realised that these unexpected braking effects were due to the links and not to some obstruction in the gearbox, the jolts became far less frightening than they were to begin with. They were a new experience which we suffered gladly, knowing that in a few more kilometres we would be riding on the smooth back of India's tarmac roads. Before this, I was to have one more great disappointment, namely Dera Ghazi Khan.

Of course I had established, as far as possible, the route we were to take before leaving home. I was able to form a picture in my mind for a good few of the place-names: Istanbul, Teheran, Agra, Bombay – I had a pretty good idea of how they might look. Sometimes the picture was far removed from reality, but somehow never absolutely wrong. There were other place names which suggested no pictures to my mind. They remained no more than stages along the way. Then there were two or three names which aroused magical expectations in me. I had read no details of these towns nor seen any photographs of them, it was simply the sound of their names which set me dreaming. It was almost like a song, or a term of endearment. Kalat Zarife! Could this name conceal only poverty-stricken mud huts? Surely it had to be a village out of *The Arabian Nights*, with a full moon shining above it, and palm-trees beneath which veiled figures darted on dainty feet like gazelles to their tryst with daring lovers. This had long been my dream, until I got to Kalat Zarife. It was nothing but a very ordinary dusty village halfway down the Euphrates, and a total disappointment to me.

Another name along our route to tickle the imagination was Dera Ghazi Khan. It had a harder, more severe ring to it and made me think of venerable white-bearded old men, of stern mosques and pretty temples, of eternal blue skies and lush jungle vegetation. Now we were coming to this town.

Dera Ghazi Khan's vegetation was rather more sparse than in Kufstein, and the sky above us was a leaden grey. At the same time, it was as hot as the finest days in Arabia. There were neither mosques nor temples, at least, not on the main streets, but only miserable modern brick buildings with corrugated iron roofs and garish shop fronts. Instead of the venerable whitebeards I had expected to greet us with a courteous wave of the hand, and an invitation to sit down in the shade with them to sip coffee, we were met on the very outskirts of the town by a horde of adolescent boys, who ran alongside, behind and in front of us, sweating, shouting and smelling of garlic. Their numbers grew rapidly, and with their numbers their audacity. At first their curiosity only led them to grab at the shiny parts of the machine; then at our legs; then even at our faces. The only gratifying bit was when, in their enthusiasm, they grabbed at the cylinder and the exhaust pipe and gave up the pursuit with a shriek of pain. But for every one who got burnt, two new warriors leapt into the breach. It was most unpleasant.

We had to de-coke the engine and looked for a mechanic's workshop. Soon we found one and got to work. I will never forget the hour that followed. Our horde of pursuers had found us out. They pressed around us so closely that we could not move. Only when Herbert or I got angry and swore at them did they inch back a little. We had to make the best use we could of these few seconds to make the movements necessary for the job while we had the space, for the circle would soon close up tight again. The English speak of the 'teeming millions' of Asia. This expression loses something of its meaning when translated into German, and we had often thought it somewhat contemptuous and spiteful. We now understood its deeper meaning, for we ourselves were in contact with a fraction of those teeming millions. We *did* feel a little contempt, because the young lads were dirty, unwashed

The first motorcycle on the land route to India; the first time that Europe and India were linked by motor transport. There were reports in the Indian press and in many newspapers around the world about the beginning of a new era of motor transport in Asia. The land route of Alexander the Great, the legendary caravan road which Sven Hedin had rediscovered, was now recalled to life in the age of the motor engine.

*143*

and rude, but there was a bit of instinctive fear mixed up in it as well, because there were so many of them, they didn't care, and there were only two of us. In this one hour in the workshop at Dera Ghazi Khan we learned a whole lot about colonial psychology. Until now we had approached all 'natives' in a friendly spirit and had never treated them arrogantly. We had always got along fine like this, but now for the first time, we felt obliged to employ 'colonial' methods to protect ourselves from being overwhelmed by a superior force. We shouted at them and they laughed cheekily back. They exchanged hilarious and uninhibited remarks about our language, our faces, our skin and our hair. There was nothing about us which they did not find ridiculous to the last degree. When we rode on, they accompanied us in a howling pack and we were heartily glad to leave the last corrugated iron roofs of Dera Ghazi Khan well behind us.

Immediately after this, we crossed the Indus, the river bed being several kilometres wide at this point. However, the great volumes of water from the summer monsoon had long since rushed down towards the sea, flooding the land with terror, destruction and new life. The land was arid and dusty now, even the river bed was an arid desert, white as snow, with only three pathetic watercourses left to remind us that here was one of the greatest rivers of India. After its long journey from the high plains of Tibet, through the mighty gorges of the Himalaya, after many hundreds of kilometres through Indian heat and drought, it was tired now and flowing gently to its destination. We crossed the three channels by ferry and soon found ourselves in the midst of fertile agricultural land. Crossing the river had taken only an hour. Had we attempted the same manœuvre during the rainy season, it would have taken us one or two days of hard, dangerous work. The waters might well have been so swollen that we would never have got near the true course of the river, or the boatmen might have put us off, saying, "We cannot go this week. Maybe next week or the week after, if the rain and meltwaters have gone. You must wait, sahibs."

But we did not have to wait. Luck was with us again, we had arrived at the right moment, and a good road took us on through Multan to Lahore, the most important city in north-west India.

This was another world. The adventurous part of our journey which had actually begun in the Balkans, with bad roads and the difficulty of finding our way, in fact everything that had cost us so many anxious hours, was now over. Here were excellent tarmac roads and excellent signposts giving the distances. Of course, we realised later that Indian roads are only excellent when they are leading to or going through, strategically important areas. But even in places where only peasants or pilgrims use them, they are still good. Difficulties for the motorcyclist had shrunk almost to nothing and we could now spend all our time concentrating on the magical aspects of our surroundings.

When I read through the old reports that we sent to the newspapers at that time, I keep coming across the word 'magical.' Our articles were surprisingly popular with readers because we gave them the picture they wanted of a magical land which they would probably never get to see in reality. I don't believe that either of us at that time knew enough literary psychology to be influenced by this. Probably we were just so young and enthusiastic that we saw most things as if they came out of a fairytale anyway, and that is how we described them.

Since then I have crossed India again, going from the Khyber Pass to Assam; Herbert has lived in India for a year, and we have both wondered why it seemed so magical to us then. Of course there are many places in India, and buildings and landscapes that merit this description. Then again, India has the Taj-Mahal, the most beautiful building in the world. But everyday India is monotonous, sad and poor. Wide areas of meagre grassland with a few tall trees, not enough to call a forest, poverty-stricken villages, all with low mud houses and a dirty pond on the outskirts (a breeding ground for malaria), and the buffalo with their herd boys. Any landscape in Central Europe is lovelier than the greater part of India.

India is not one and the same throughout, it is a continent full of cultural and geographical contrasts. Thus, many experts on the country may find fault with my judgment and so I had better qualify it straight away. It only applies to the landscape along the main roads from Lahore to Bombay and Lahore to Calcutta. If you have ever seen the Himalaya, whether or not you care about mountains in general, the sight of it will haunt you for ever. Coming from the heat of the Indian plain, you approach the foothills. Here, about 2000 metres up are situated the famous hill station resorts such as Dera Dun, Mussorie, Naini Tai and Darjeeling. You are in hill country with a mixture of tropical and alpine flora. You have left the oppressive heat of the plain behind, and the mornings and evenings are fresh and cool. Then, on a particularly clear day, you will see in the north a long, thin cloud hanging in the air, the only cloud in a completely dark-blue sky. The cloud will be unchanged hours later, and although you know what it is, you can't believe it: this cloud is the peaks of the Himalaya. They hang so high up and so far above the spectator that you are constantly deluded into thinking that it is a cloud. If you travel nearer, the white streak breaks up into individual peaks, an improbable harmony of great bold shapes. If you have seen this, you may be forgiven for the generalisation that India is magical.

Lahore was a beautiful and orderly town. I say 'was' advisedly, since the fighting between Moslems and Hindus in 1946 and 1947 caused great devastation. There was once a bazaar overflowing with people and glorious with colour, where you could buy anything produced in Europe and Asia – fabrics from England, silk from Kashmir, tea from China, iron and steel goods from Germany, light bulbs and bicycles from Japan. You could look round it for hours and witness a vivid cross-section of Asia's economic history.

Apart from the bazaar, there was the exclusive residential area, housing the Europeans and rich Indians – wide shady streets with beautifully kept gardens where bungalows stood under tall cool trees. We had a letter of introduction to Dr GJ Sondhi, secretary of the Indian Olympic Committee, and we were not a little surprised when the first Indian we asked for directions to Dr Sondhi's said without thinking, "Oh, you want the Professor, you must go to the university quarter." We received similarly prompt answers to our subsequent questions. Sondhi seemed to be a well-known character in the city.

He was also an outstandingly clever one. As a professor of history who had taken his degree in England and who was well-acquainted with Europe and America, he was a fine judge of world events. I can remember a conversation we had in Lahore that seemed quite absurd to me at the time. Sondhi was looking forward to a year's sabbatical in 1939. We tried to persuade him to spend it in Europe, promising to show him the sights of Austria.

"I should love to come to Europe," said Sondhi, "but who knows how much will be left of that continent in six years time?"

We stared at him in amazement. Did he mean an earthquake? This seemed a more likely danger, to our minds, than war. Then Sondhi explained his fears. With the clear knowledge of a specialist and his Asian point of view sharpened by remoteness, both physical and psychological, he perceived the developments in Europe as threatening and dangerous. We were amused then by his fears, but he was absolutely right with his vision of the Second World War. I hope this recollection may serve as an example of the sort of intelligent and liberal-minded people we often met in India. Our impatient arrogance in Dera Ghazi Khan was forgotten now, and made way for quite the opposite feeling.

Sondhi lived opposite the university in a beautiful bungalow. He welcomed us warmly, and his wife, who spoke fluent English just as he did, was a charming elegant person. Suddenly a man from the press turned up and we had to get back on the bike and shake Sondhi by the hand. The next morning this picture, together with a detailed description of the route by which we had come appeared in all Lahore's newspapers. As a consequence, we received so many invitations that we would probably still be in India today if we had accepted them all. Perhaps people who called India a magical land were considering it from the point of view of hospitality.

A colossal tent was erected for us in Sondhi's garden, containing a living room and a bedroom. Somewhat in the background and nearly in the bushes stood another modest little tent, whose purpose I need not dwell on at any length. Once you have got used to it, living in a tent offers unsuspected pleasures, especially in a land where accommodation in buildings is often not particularly clean. Sven Hedin, in the course of his journey, often preferred even in big cities to put up his tent in a garden, and the late Sir Aurel Stein who achieved great things as an archaeologist in Central Asia, lived, or in his case one may truly say 'stayed,' by choice for years at a time under canvas in Kashmir. In our tent we were undisturbed, and what is more, we did not disturb Sondhi's household. We had electric light, of course, and an electric fan.

Our stream of visitors included students from the university. They were eager for knowledge, very friendly and ready to show us anything we wanted to see, although it was difficult for us to be on equally good terms with all of them. All of them, however, were enthusiastic supporters of Gandhi and, if one could believe what they said, their most earnest desire was the abolition of the caste system. But, if we went out one day with Hindus, then the next day the Moslems would be disgruntled, and *vice versa*. At the university there were separate dormitories and dining rooms for the followers of each religion. The dining rooms in particular were situated far away from each other, for it would be all too easy for some Hindu hothead to realise that the flesh of the sacred cow was being eaten here and be inspired to commit a spontaneous act of protest, or more likely a deliberate one, with dire consequences. For the Moslems, the Hindu pork-eating habit is no less abominable. A minor religious brawl amongst the students might spread like wildfire through the whole city, with incalculable results. These were the facts of the situation, a pathetic contrast with the enthusiastic theoretical declarations of young idealists who,

Arriving in Lahore, being greeted by the president of the Indian Olympic Committee Dr Sondhi and his wife. The picture appeared in many newspapers around the world, as it really was the first time that a motorcycle had conquered the land route to India.

wishing to show their country to foreigners in the best light, probably persuaded themselves of their own goodwill.

It was now the end of October, and so, after several delightful days, we rode off along the excellent 'Great Trunk Road' towards our other destinations. The names promised so much: Delhi, Agra, Bombay! Our thoughts of Bombay were already beginning to be tinged with sadness. For many weeks it had been just an exotic sound, somewhere impossibly far away. We would often say, "When we get to Bombay ... " and let ourselves imagine all sorts of wonderful things. Bombay seemed so distant and so improbable that any of our dreams might come true there. Now Bombay had become a reality. "When you get to Bombay, you must visit my nephew," said a well-meaning Indian, and a motoring enthusiast thought that if we kept going, we could be there in five days. We were horrified: only five days and our journey would be over! We decided definitely against 'keeping going.' We had not come to India merely to go racing through it.

As a parting gift, Sondhi gave us a valuable *kris*, inlaid with ivory, which was intended to protect us on the rest of our journey.

"We shall be perfectly all right," we said, "as long as the machine holds out."

"For that, I have an infallible talisman!" laughed Sondhi, and he gave us a tiny ball of ivory no bigger than a pea. This ball could be unscrewed, and inside it were six microscopic hand carved elephants, symbols of strength and endurance.

# 17

# HOW WE LOST FACE IN THE GOLDEN TEMPLE

We were on our way yet again. It was a pleasure now. We flew along the wonderful tarmac road as if in a dream, and found it hard to remember all the weary kilometres in Baluchistan.

Sometimes the road took us through grassland and fields, then it would again be lined with trees. The sight of monkeys was still new to us, and we often stopped and tried to entice them to come near, but they were enraged by this unexpected interest and fled back into the tops of the trees and palms, cursing and chattering. Only when we rode on did they come swinging down to earth and laugh at our retreating backs. As well as monkeys, there were hordes of squirrels living along the road. They didn't look quite the same as our squirrels in Austria, but they were every bit as agile and good climbers. One of their favourite tricks was to dash across the road right in front of the machine as it roared by. It seemed to be a question of life and death: the ones on the left hand side of the road were obsessed with getting over to the right and the ones on the right with getting over to the left, even if they could only manage it with less than a foot to spare as the front wheel bore down on them. Hundreds of times we thought we were going to kill these little animals, but in fact, we never ran over a single one. It was really just a harmless little game they were playing, but it certainly played on our nerves.

Dr Sondhi had telephoned to a relative in Amritsar to announce our arrival. The way Dr Sondhi never thought twice about telephoning to Delhi, Agra or any other city a few hundred or even over a thousand kilometres away, demonstrated to us that in many technical matters India had caught up with the West.

Luck was with us, and we arrived in Amritsar at just the right time for the big Sikh celebrations which are held there annually. We had known very little about the Sikhs until now, although we had already seen many of them. They were hefty farmers and industrious businessmen, but our knowledge of the sect was confined to a warning from one of the Moslem students not to ask a Sikh the time in the middle of the day. The reasoning behind this was as follows: on religious grounds, Sikhs are forbidden to cut the hair or beard. As it grows very strongly, the hair of their head is thick and reaches down to the knee, and their beards are not much shorter. The hair is twisted up and kept under a turban and the beard is rolled up under the chin.

Their face is thus surrounded by great masses of hair. There is a spiteful popular tradition that when the sun is highest at midday and at its hottest, Sikhs are not quite right in the head. This explains why we were warned not to ask strapping great Sikhs cheeky questions about the time.

In Amritsar, the Sikhs' religious and political centre, we soon learned more about this strange religious group. The word 'Sikh' means disciple, and the first Sikhs gathered around Nanak, the founder of their religion, who was born in the Punjab in 1469. He belonged to a lowly Hindu caste and devoted himself to studying the ancient doctrines of the Vedas and also the more mystical commandments of the Koran. He did not found a new religion but became, rather like Luther in Europe and Tsongkapa in Tibet, a reformer of existing doctrine. He rejected, among other things, the law of caste, the worship of idols, and pilgrimages. The cow is also sacred to Sikhs, and corpses are cremated according to the same rites used by Hindus. The only idol they revere is the Holy Book, a collection of hymns and prayers by their leaders, known as *gurus*. The festival, which coincided with our arrival in Amritsar, celebrates the birthday of their founder, Guru Nanak.

Sondhi's relative, himself a Hindu and not a Sikh, gave us a long and detailed description of this not only very pious, but also warlike community. During cruel persecution under the Moslem Mughals, Sikhs formed themselves into warrior bands. They added to their names the designation *Singh,* meaning 'lion,' considering it the greatest honour. With the courage that so often distinguishes militant religious movements, they not only repulsed attacks from the Mughals in the south and the Afghans in the west, but founded an independent empire centring on Amritsar, which was only broken up by the British. Along with the Gurkhas and the Pathans (neither of which are from India proper, but from border territories, the former from Nepal and the latter from the Afghan border), they are deemed the best soldiers in India. Today they are found in astonishing numbers in work which demands a sense of order and reliability. In Hong Kong, Shanghai, Tientsin and other cities of South-east Asia which rely heavily on British capital, it is principally Sikhs who find employment as traffic police and night porters.

As we approached the temple and saw the faithful, we found it impossible to connect these dignified figures with their humdrum employment. But earning one's daily bread and praying to the gods on a feast-day are two radically different things. Every old Sikh was transformed into a great patriarch, every child into an enchanted prince or princess, as the case might be – and the Sikh ladies looked like big flowers lavishly created from Nature's magic palette. It was truly a bewitching spectacle.

In the course of our trip we had already seen a number of outstandingly beautiful buildings – Hagia Sophia in Istanbul, the mosques of Baghdad and Meshed, the old gateways of Teheran, the Mughal tombs at Lahore, and many others, but none of them took our breath away quite like the Golden Temple. Maybe it was because the view we remember was early in the day, as the sun's slanting rays were just penetrating the morning mist, and the architectural details were not obliterated in a blaze of light, but picked out delicately and softly, as if illuminated from within. Maybe it was also because we were infected with the crowd's mood of religious solemnity. At that moment we would have sworn on oath that men had built nothing more beautiful on the face of the earth. That was before we saw the Taj Mahal. For now, we stood before the Golden Temple of the Sikhs at Amritsar, in ecstasy, bereft of speech.

It had not been altogether easy to attain this state of ecstasy. Sikhs in general are a tolerant people, not as arrogant as the Brahmins who looked at us as if we were the dregs of humanity. But Sikhs also had their strict rules. Before entering the temple area, not only did we have to remove our shoes, as in most other shrines, but we had to wash our feet into the bargain. At first we thought this must be an extra precaution taken against us as Europeans, whose purity was apparently always in question, but to our relief we observed that everyone who came in was obliged to submit to this procedure. We felt ourselves on equal terms again and were able to hold up our heads which had been drooping in shame (if such a thing is possible while you are washing your feet and about five hundred Sikhs are watching with big dark eyes to see whether you are washing thoroughly enough). At last we were ready and were pushed forward by the crowd.

Then came our humiliation. We made to go through a gateway where other believers were passing in and out. We were politely but firmly stopped by an old Sikh.

"Have you got anything to smoke?" he asked in very good English.

"Yes," I said and offered him my cigarettes. A horrified expression crossed his face. I was ashamed, as they were the cheapest brand to be bought in the bazaar and he was a very old gentleman.

The jostling crowd at the entrance to the Golden Temple of the Sikhs in Amritsar. It was here that we experienced an embarrassing search for forbidden alcohol and tobacco.

"Have you, perhaps ... ?" I said, turning to Herbert. He felt in his pockets and produced a very nice cigar. Where on earth..? Ah yes, our host at supper last night had offered us cigars.

The old gentleman said politely, but quite coldly, "Will you please leave all tobacco products here. When you leave, you may take them with you."

Abashed, we made a little heap of our tobacco products. My cigarettes, Herbert's cigar, a second cigar. Herbert then produced a third. Well, well! It was a good thing that it was not our host but his servant who had brought us to the temple.

We had lost a lot of 'face' and were not at all surprised when the old Sikh asked, "Are you carrying any alcohol?"

I shook my head energetically. Then I remembered that we had drunk a lot of whisky the previous evening. Suppose Herbert ... ? In all my life I have never felt so wretched as I did then, when the old gentleman began to feel our pockets carefully, first mine, then Herbert's. Herbert made a guilty face. My brain began to work overtime: on our going to bed the night before, our host had pressed us to take anything with us that might help us sleep easily – cigars, whisky, fruit, scented candles. We had pointedly refused the scented candles, but that was all. If Herbert had responded to our host's suggestion of cigars, it was scarcely to be hoped that he had refused the alcohol. Even if he only had a half-empty bottle of whisky on him, the crowd would be unlikely to let it go quietly. They were already looking less kindly on us. They would regard us as desecrators of the temple, for, as we now saw, tobacco and alcohol were banned in Sikh daily life, and if any were found in the vicinity of a shrine, this would constitute a crime. They would tear us in pieces or at least give us a good thrashing. Then the servant who accompanied us would inform his master that a riot had started over cigars and whisky. Dr Sondhi would hear of it, and inform his colleague the secretary of the Austrian Olympic Committee in Vienna and we would be the cause of a diplomatic incident between India and Austria.

All this flashed through my mind in the few seconds that it took the temple guardian to search Herbert. Then he stood up and bowed politely. "Be so good as to collect your ... " he hesitated for a moment as if searching for the right word, ... "your *things* from here when you leave the temple."

We bowed and went on our way.

"Why didn't he find it?" I asked Herbert.

"Find what?" he asked, sounding offended.

"The whisky," I whispered.

"You mean you thought ..."

"I was afraid you'd ..."

"The bottle was too big," said Herbert, "I left it at home."

"We're going to need it," I said, wiping the sweat from my forehead.

But our fears were at an end, and now began one of the most beautiful and brilliantly colourful days of our trip.

# 18

# GRASS FIRES AND A GUILTY CONSCIENCE

Meanwhile, the sun had risen higher, although it had not yet reached full strength, and shadows were long. The temple's golden roof gleamed like an enormous jewel against the blue sky, and its reflection lay quietly like a soft pearl in the water of the lake. Every detail of the image could be seen, but as soon as the faithful stepped down into the holy water to begin pouring it over themselves, the outlines grew blurred and the water changed to golden lava.

Even though the Sikhs worship no idols, their Holy Book has almost become one. They handle it with a reverence otherwise paid only to gods. On this day and the one following, the ceremony demanded that it should be read aloud without interruption for a full forty-eight hours. Only the most worthy members of the community are enlisted to perform this sacred task, which they do by turns. The reader sat on the podium, his voice droning monotonously across the wide square in front of the building.

As is often the case in Asia, here too there was a mixture of genuine harmonious beauty and tacky modern kitsch. The adjustable electric desk lamp would not have disgraced any office, but it seemed out of place in the lavishly gilded and bejewelled temple. So did the tin clock with an alarm bell, such as you find in every kitchen back home, presumably intended to remind the reader when he was due to be relieved.

This predilection for clocks is a strange thing. Clocks are to be found in all sorts of unsuitable places, but never in the places they are needed, such as railway stations. Favourite sites are temples, or other shrines remarkable for their timeless atmosphere. Clocks stand under the Wheel of Life, and beneath Buddha's compassionate smile. They stand still, certainly not going, since clockmakers are rarer than monks hereabouts, and the busy ticking soon falls silent. If the new Indian government ever has such a thing as a Ministry of Culture, then there is a great opportunity here for some welcome legislation.

However, we did not let ourselves be carried away by such details. It was the whole picture that remained unforgettable – the blue sky, the glistening roof, and their reflection in the still waters, the crowd in festive attire, where the white of the men's clothing predominated, interspersed with the lovely hues of the women's saris. When we returned late that afternoon to our host's home, we were convinced that we had experienced the high point of our trip.

Tired and happy, we luxuriated on our camp-beds, smoking the cigars which the old gentleman had not forgotten to return to us. Our heads were still swimming with the brilliant kaleidoscope of colours and the roof of the temple flaming gold against the sky.

"I'm so glad we got photographs," said Herbert, "or they'd never believe us at home."

"We very nearly didn't," I said, reliving once more the worst moment of the festival. I had just got the Leica to my eye and was trying to capture a really good shot, when I felt a sharp blow on my chin and the camera went flying up in the air. For a moment I saw only a clenched fist and an angry young face, then my attention was riveted on the camera. We were standing on a very hard floor of marble tiles. If it hit the ground here, it would be useless. The camera was still sailing overhead like a strange oval ball, so I leapt over a couple of bystanders, charged after it like practised goalkeeper and got it safe in my hands. In football jargon this is known as a 'brilliant save.' Not only the camera was saved: Herbert said it made his hair stand on end as he watched. Only another couple of feet and I would have ended up, together with the camera, taking a dip in the holy lake. The faithful may have found the lake very attractive for bathing, and we thought it was lovely to look at, but as for actually going in – no thank you. Seen close to, the water was greyish green.

So I lay on the lakeside awaiting the next shock, but saw only a few kindly old faces peering down at me. I was helped up, and another English-speaking Sikh was soon on the scene. He apologised profusely for the young hothead who had stopped me taking a picture. "These young people ... " he explained, rebuking them. Then other gentlemen arrived and we found ourselves at the centre of a friendly gathering, everyone asking our forgiveness. We were only too ready to give it. The odd thing was that in the course of explanations, they kept on insisting that if the young man had only known that we were *Austrians*, then he would never have let himself be carried away, but he had thought we were English. Since we could scarcely believe that he had any special affection for Austria, we could only assume that for England the opposite applied. Whatever the case, after this we were almost obliged to take more pictures than we really wanted.

This camera of mine certainly had an eventful trip! After all the curses I had heaped on it in the watchmaker's shop in Teheran, I had nevertheless managed to repair it, and it then became a faithful travelling companion and a hardy survivor of all dangers. Once it fell in the water, and only – would you believe it? – in drought-stricken Baluchistan, in the one and only well, or to be more exact the only waterhole that we came across. After trying unsuccessfully to drink the water, which was like lye, we rested there for a bit and also took a few pictures. We were tired and lying on the sand and the camera was standing on a block of stone, a good metre away from the waterhole. Then there was a sudden gust of wind, one of those violent atmospheric disturbances that are peculiar to the desert. There had been not a breath of wind, and then came a howling that bore down on us like a whistling express train, swept over us, whirling sand and stones into the air and vanished as abruptly as it had come. We clamped our hands over our faces to protect our eyes from the worst of the sand and our heads from flying stones, and when I looked up again, the camera was gone. It was lying at the bottom of the shallow water so I fetched it back on to dry land and laid it carefully down, feeling the same as I would for a friend who had had an accident. In only a few minutes it was completely dry and I was able to scrape away the salt. After this, it took appreciably better photographs. I informed Herr Leitz and promptly got a letter back, saying that his technicians absolutely refused to believe the salt water bath theory, but thanking me for my valuable observation.

Then came the experience in the Golden Temple at Amritsar, and, a little later, only a few kilometres before we got to Bombay, our ways nearly parted for ever – mine and the camera's, that is. We had passed the night at the roadside in our tent, and, in the morning, we nearly caused a small disaster. The landscape was rolling steppe with the Ghats in the background, like the mountains of the Holy Grail. The steppe grass was tall and very dry. I must emphasise again, in order to explain what happened next, that we were children. We behaved like children, anyway.

Herbert began by saying, "This grass would burn very easily."

"A good thing we haven't got anything we want to cook," I replied.

"True," said Herbert, "but it would have made an interesting picture – the motorcycle in the foreground with the burning steppe in the background."

Of course, that was a splendid idea. I had made it a point of honour to bring back interesting pictures which could be used for publicity. A burning steppe was not such a bad notion. Perhaps I might be able to ride through the fire at some point where it had stopped burning and was just smoking. The directors would be most enthusiastic.

"We'll light this patch of grass," I said, "and when it's burning, I'll ride past it. Take my yellow filter so that you get a good shot of the white smoke clouds."

Herbert got his camera ready, I put mine down on the roadside and we lit the grass.

Something completely unexpected happened. We had thought that the gentle breeze would spread the weak flame a bit, just enough for us to throw some more grass over it and create smoke. That is what we thought, but we had no experience of Indian grass in the dry season. At first, for one or two quiet seconds, there really was just a little flame, then the wind got up. It whistled, hissed, crackled, and we were confronted with a wall of fire several metres high. Burning tufts of grass flew through the air and we were surrounded by a sea of fire. I think Karl May must have had something similar in mind with that exceptionally effective description of the burning savannah, but I hope for his sake that he never came as near to it as we did. This seems unlikely, seeing that the grass in Radebeul (May's home) near Dresden is rather juicy.

We forgot all about taking photographs and could think of nothing else but escape. The machine was already running and with one bound we were both on it and away. Only when we'd gone about a kilometre did we stop to look round. A thick dark cloud of smoke was rising skywards. At ground level there was a fiery yellow flicker. We sped on.

We were very dejected all day. Our guilty conscience led us to imagine the dreadful consequences that would descend on us: arrest, prosecution, hostile newspaper reports under the headline 'Two Austrian globetrotters wreak havoc.' It wasn't just the fire that weighed on our minds, but a small thing that had caused us much amusement over the last few days – dodging the tolls. The roads hereabouts were again mostly in very bad condition, so we resented being stopped every few kilometres by an Indian who was usually bad-tempered, and having to pay a few *annas* road toll. It wasn't so much the money we resented as the principle. We had paid nothing on the superb tarmac roads of Northern India, so why should we suddenly pay now, for this dubious pleasure? We did not stop to think that our payments would in all probability be used to transform these bumpy roads into smooth tarmac in their turn. We merely felt cheated, and so we began to dodge them. We would freewheel up to the toll keeper, who was armed with nothing but a red flag, as if we had the money ready in our hands. On reaching him, we would swerve closely around him and make off at full throttle. Some of the toll keepers were left standing stock-still, others waved their flags desperately and one even threw stones after us. He was a good shot and the stones narrowly missed Herbert's head. Herbert was the one who put the case for greater compliance with the law, but generally only where the road gradient prevented high speeds. Now all these sins returned to haunt us.

This was not a good day. In the evening, as we were asking a farmer to put us up for the night, I noticed that I no longer had the camera: it had been left behind at the site of the arson.

Anything else could go wrong, I thought, but I would have that camera. It was pointless to run away from what we'd done. Too many farmers had turned to look at our motorcycle and the newspapers in Bombay were already expecting our arrival. It was simpler for a camel to go through the eye of a needle than for us to disappear, so, the following morning, we went back.

"At least we can't miss the place," said Herbert, trying to make a joke of it, "Where it's all black, that's where your camera is lying in the ditch."

We had been going a few minutes when a dreadful sight met our eyes – a thick cloud of smoke. Could the fire have spread for more than a hundred kilometres? I have never felt guiltier in all my life, but I rode on. There was nothing to be done now. At the site of the fire we saw several farmers fighting the flames. But no, they were feeding them, and really taking a lot of trouble over it. In places where the fire went out, they lit it again. We stopped and addressed them in broken Hindustani. They said they were indeed burning the grass. Grass was a bad thing and had to be burned to discourage tigers and other noxious animals, so that the farmers could cultivate the land. This day and the previous one had been perfect for such work. The grass was dry and the wind just strong enough. We would see fires like this all along the road, and were not to worry. It happened every winter and was quite normal. This was a great load off our minds and we sang as we went on our way.

But the singing didn't last long. We passed so many burning places and they all looked exactly alike. How were we to find the place where we had camped? Our odometer had been on strike for several days so we did not know exactly how far we had travelled the day before. It was moreover an exceptionally monotonous landscape, rolling steppe on both sides of the road with just the magical mountain peaks on the far horizon.

But we had set our minds on the thing and were not going to give up lightly. For two days we searched the lightly charred roadside ditches and looked dirtier than we had at any time on our journey, which is saying something, and it enhanced the adventurous impression we gave on our arrival in Bombay. Just as we were at the end of our tether and ready to kiss goodbye to the camera, there it was, lying innocently before us, quite unscathed. Even the grass surrounding it had not been burned – the wind had carried the fire away from the camera.

The Indian waste disposal service (a flock of vultures) descending on a dead ox. After a few hours, only the bare bones are left. A sure way of avoiding epidemics.

*VISIT VELOCE ON THE WEB – WWW.VELOCE.CO.UK*
*All current books • New book news • Special offers • Gift vouchers • Forum*

*156*

# 19

# VAIKUNTH
# HEAVEN ON EARTH

Our next destination was the princely state of Patiala where we had an invitation from the Maharajah. Now I write this, it seems rather as if we cadged our way all through India, as there were invitations waiting for us in nearly every state. This was not really our fault. India is a very hospitable country. With no more than one or two friends, you are unlikely to stay in an hotel.

"Are you going to Agra?" a friend would ask, "In that case you must stay with my Uncle Muckerji."

Uncle Muckerji then sends you to his friend Ranjit Singh in Dholpur, who sends you on to a Mr Gokhale in Bhopal. Thus you get passed from hand to hand and of course learn far more about the country and its people than by staying in a series of hotels. There is only one drawback to this chain of hospitality. If it is begun by a Hindu, then one can be fairly sure that all the other links will be Hindus too. If a Moslem is the first to take you in, then all subsequent hosts arranged by him will be Moslems too. "India is one" proclaimed the politicians' banners, but in those days, as now, there were different Indias which paid no attention to one another, at least no friendly attention.

The Maharajah's invitation lay outside both these spheres. Since he was president of the Indian Olympic Committee, it was, so to speak, a formal invitation. He seemed to regard it as such, anyway, since we only saw him face to face quite briefly. He had more important and pleasurable things to do than converse with passing motorcyclists. As head of the Indian Chamber of Princes, he played an important part in political life. He was a keen sportsman and would happily fly a few thousand kilometres in one of his five aircraft in order to watch an interesting cricket match. In his own state he held unlimited powers of life and death. If protests were occasionally raised at his dictatorial measures, he was adept at buying silence. He was a figure from the feudal Middle Ages, transposed with all the attendant glitter and cruelty into the present day.

We were housed in one of the guest palaces. To begin with, we were bewildered by the suite of luxurious apartments placed at our disposal, but compared with the palace of the Maharajah himself, ours was a modest little hut. There was yet another palace. From the outside it looked forbidding and severe, like an elegant prison and this was where the Maharajah's wives were housed. There were five principal wives, the Maharanees A, B, C, D and E, supplemented by another two hundred concubines, about whose nationality rumours were rife. The composition of the household was said to reflect the Maharajah's cosmopolitan outlook, and as the British took a strong line regarding relationships between white women and Indians, the Maharajah was said to have experienced difficulties on several occasions. Even for the British Secret Service, it cannot have been easy to penetrate the secrets of the women's palace. It was by no means the pushover that we were – a couple of glasses of whisky rendered us garrulous and communicative.

Reading Kipling's *Kim*, especially the instruction which Kim receives on how to strengthen his powers of observation and memory, had raised the Secret Service to legendary status in my eyes. Its agents were playing such a bold game, and for the highest stakes! And what a mighty field it was where they played: from the icy passes of the Himalaya to the teeming bazaars of the south! I had very romantic notions about their activity. Then I met the friendly old gentlemen whose job it was to find out whether we were planning a revolution in India. At this point, I learned that it was also part of my heroes' duties to ascertain the nationality of whichever lady shared the Maharajah's bed each night. My idols fell from their pedestals! But I was too hasty in my judgment. A little later I heard a story which, if true, could stand alongside *Kim*.

The Secret Service had learned that an Indian nationalist organisation was planning to murder the governor of the Punjab. One of its agents, an Englishman with a perfect command of several Indian dialects, was charged with breaking up the conspiracy. He disguised himself as an Indian, rented a stall in the bazaar at Lahore and soon managed to gain the confidence of the terrorists. Not only this, but he even became a leading figure within the conspiracy. When he had gathered enough evidence, he had the conspirators arrested. They still had no idea that their talented leader was himself a member of the same British police who carried out this operation. Throughout the entire process, they all remained faithful to the man who purported to be their friend and nobody betrayed him. They probably hoped that he would carry on and complete their interrupted task. It is said that when the same man appeared as their prosecutor in court, they were greatly ashamed of their own negligence but also greatly amazed at the British achievement. The hero of the action was transferred quietly to other duties – it seems that the Secret Service does not care for heroes and probably does not mind being made fun of. Having heard this story, I never made fun of the Service again.

While we were in Patiala, we wanted to make an excursion to the Himalaya. We were still quite near to the mountains here and they were almost within reach, although our way onward lay to the south. This was our last opportunity if we wanted to breathe cool fresh mountain air once again. We also had a letter of introduction in our pocket which now seemed well worth having. Herbert had got it in Vienna many months back from a journalist who had just returned from India, and while he was there he had spent several enjoyable weeks with a German forester somewhere in the Himalaya. Our project had not been finalised at the time, and Herbert had accepted the letter without attaching any great significance to it. Now we extracted it from amongst our papers and realised that 'somewhere in the Himalaya' was only a few hours away from Patiala by car and that the forester Johannssen was an employee of the Maharajah.

So we went north, first crossing the plain, which was flat and monotonous, devoid of any magical charms, poverty-stricken, hungry and backward, although the wretched mud huts radiated a certain appeal, as did the lazy, contented water-buffalo and their inquisitive herd boys. Then the plain rose slowly but steadily, so gradually and so evenly that we would scarcely have noticed the change if the machine had not laboured more heavily. The Himalaya, at least according to geologists, is still growing and is pulling the plain up with it where the two meet. In Kalka, a small township, we reached the boundary between the plain and the mountains, which was quite clearly marked. The southern half of the village has all the characteristics of a settlement on the plain, and the northern was already built like a mountain village. We rode into Kalka in third gear (top) and left again in first on a steep mountain road.

Now followed one of the loveliest parts of our trip. In Persia and Baluchistan the mountains had been more massive, but they had not risen so dramatically out of the plain. Also they had been dry and bare, but here they were richly clothed with vegetation which altered gradually. At the foot of the mountains it was lush and tropical, then it became Mediterranean with many cacti and evergreen trees, then it lost its southern character and became more reminiscent of Central Europe with its huge conifers and shady deciduous forests. The air changed gradually in the same way: at first there was tropical heat, then it became pleasantly mild and finally tangy and fresh. If you press on further into the mountains to the north, and our destination lay in the conifer and deciduous forests, then you reach the climate and flora of our own Alps and finally the glacial zone. The roads do not go as far as this, but end at the mountain resorts where rich Indians and Europeans go in an attempt to avoid the heat of the plain.

Only once was our attention distracted from the mountains by a very strange sight. Near the road stood an encampment of Indian gipsies. Outside one of the tents a child of about two years old was rolling happily about in the dust with little cries, enjoying the sunshine. A huge python wound itself about the child in what seemed to us deadly coils. We stopped, and hearing voices in the tent, we shouted as hard as our lungs could bear, "A snake! Save the child!"

Two gipsies came into the open and stared at us and the motorcycle with friendly smiles. We pointed in horror at the child and the snake. Still smiling and full of paternal pride they watched the ill-assorted pair at their feet and turned to us again with an air of expectation.

We were just thinking what brutes they were, when our thoughts were cut short in amazement. The child had begun, clumsily and awkwardly, to wriggle away over the snake and the snake was using its powerful body to push it back into its old place. The child got cross and pummelled the snake's body with its clenched fists. The snake, scarcely noticing this abuse, landed the child a gentle slap with its tail on the very place which a father's hand might have selected for the same purpose. We realised that our horror was out of place and that the snake was exercising parental duties towards the child, preventing it from crawling off on risky excursions away from the tent. Herr Johannssen explained to us later that gipsies in India also earn their living as entertainers and frequently keep trained pythons. In the evenings, these perform tricks before an audience, but in the daytime they have to carry out many of the duties of a well-trained dog back home with us.

After we had recovered from our fright, we began the search for Herr Johannssen. He was said to live in the vicinity of the little Himalayan village of Solon, in a genuine forester's house bearing the name 'Vaikunth.' We asked as well as we could after the 'forest sahib' and were directed to a tiny road leading away from the main road up into the mountains. We stopped outside a number of houses which seemed like a suitable abode for a European and sounded our horn, but it was always an Indian face that appeared at the window and pointed us further on.

Then something happened which I will never forget all my life.

We stopped outside another house and tooted. A girl's blonde head appeared over the balustrade of a veranda and looked at us in some surprise.

"What do you want?" asked the girl in English.

"Do you speak German?" I asked shyly.

"Of course!" said the girl. "Well, we *are* ..."

Her clear voice was interrupted by a deep impatient bass from inside the house.

"Cut the cackle, Lore. Fetch two bottles of beer, they'll be thirsty!"

As we were getting off the bike, somewhat bewildered but very happy, and the girl's head disappeared, the powerful bass voice rang out again.

"Better make it four bottles. It's very hot today."

A few minutes later we were sitting with the Johannssen family in a cool room with a cuckoo clock ticking and a huge pair of antlers overhead, leaving not the slightest doubt that we really were in the house of a German forester.

The week at 'Vaikunth' lived up to the house's name in no uncertain terms. The Indian word *Vaikunth* means something like 'heaven on earth', and that is what it was to us. We completely forgot that we were ten thousand kilometres away from home. We ate roast pork with dumplings, and fried steak with onions and potato, and Mother Johannssen, who came from North Germany, proved quick to learn the intricacies of Viennese and Tyrolean cookery. Even the language difficulties mentioned earlier concerning culinary terminology could not spoil our happiness. On Father Johannssen's birthday there were even a few bottles of Rhine wine. The formal courses of the English table which we had enjoyed at the Maharajah's now seemed much less splendid, and the strange meals we had shared with camel drivers and Indian peasants lost much of their exotic appeal. We became outright chauvinists.

The life the Johannssens were leading here in the Himalaya was truly ideal. Father Johannssen had a large field of work which was in many respects a new one. Mother Johannssen, who liked being alone, busied herself with house and kitchen, and her sole desire was to end her days here in Vaikunth. Fifteen-year-old Karlheinz had arrived from his classroom in Germany to find a genuine Paradise, from which a rather boring tutor detracted only slightly. Only twenty-year-old Lore may sometimes have felt a little lonely when she sometimes saw no other European for weeks at a time, apart from the manager of the brewery in Solon, Arthur Price, and his wife. There was indeed a real brewery in Solon where the Mid-European climate and the good water were just right for the production of beer in this otherwise miserable little place.

Several times we went hunting with Karlheinz for small animals. Porcupines, whose flesh roasted well, were his favourite game, although they were elusive, and he had once been allowed to shoot a panther as a birthday present from the Maharajah. He was a brave huntsman, although he was deeply in awe of the numerous monkeys. The Hindus of these mountains considered them sacred and so his father had forbidden him to shoot them. However, his father's prohibition was not the true reason for his fear of these comical animals. Once, in a steep and lonely part of the forest he had been unable to resist the temptation and he had shot down a little monkey which fell from the tree with cries of pain and distress. As Karlheinz was giving the poor creature the *coup de grâce*, a large crowd of monkeys gathered round him, glaring at him with faces so full of hatred that this alone was sufficient to arouse his fear. The monkeys did not stop at threatening grimaces, but began to bombard him with branches, fruit and stones. He swore that a few of them even started great pieces of rock rolling down on him and he only reached safety with great difficulty, and some cuts and bruises. The monkeys pursued him all the way home and surrounded the house for some hours. Whenever he went outside over the next few days he was soon surrounded by vindictive monkeys. He could never recall that time without a shudder. The tutor, on the other hand, remembered it with enthusiasm, because young Karlheinz had then seemed most attentive to his lessons. But as the monkeys' desire for revenge waned, so did Karlheinz' passion for learning.

Through Father Johannssen we became acquainted with the peculiarities of hunting in India. We were singularly unimpressed. The Maharajah would shortly be entertaining a number of high-ranking guests to an official hunt, and Father Johannssen was occupied with the preparations. He knew exactly how many tiger and panther there were in his area. The Maharajah had informed him that Guest Number One, a keen sportsman and exiled king of a Balkan state, must have a 'good' tiger; Guest Number Two, an English Member of Parliament, was considered eligible for an average tiger; Guest Number Three, a well-known English journalist, was only deemed to be deserving of a panther. For every hunt, the bag was allotted beforehand according to the rank of each guest and the goodwill of the Maharajah. The problem was to ensure that the animals had the least possible opportunity of disturbing these human arrangements. It was necessary to prevent a Number One guest going home without a tiger, or a Number Three guest getting his sights on anything above a panther. Since the big game animals had their own well-established pathways, it was not difficult to keep the more lowly-regarded guests away from the tigers. What was harder was to ensure that the highly-regarded ones made a kill, especially if they were only amateurs in the hunting field. Meticulous preparations virtually eliminated any risk of failure. For weeks now, through the provision of generous bait (live buffalo or goat), they had been getting the panthers and tigers into the habit of visiting certain places near trees. A safe place to sit had been constructed high up in the trees, also provided, if the guest's standing should warrant it, with a mosquito net and a small icebox.

In cases where there was some considerable doubt about the guest's ability to hit a target, the tigers were even accustomed to being illuminated. They were 'trained' to accept the petrol lamps set up nearby. There has been almost no incidence of a distinguished guest leaving Patiala without his tiger skin.

Among Indians themselves there are some very brave hunters. We heard of a

If you believe the expression of the boy on the left of the picture, then the embrace of the python may not be so harmless after all.

Maharajah (of Alwar, I think) who only shot his tigers from ground level. He even scorned hunting by elephant, which is dangerous enough. He would go stalking all day through long grass where beaters knew there was a tiger, and then usually it took no more than a fraction of a second to decide which became the prey – the hunter or his quarry. This Maharajah is said to have shot several hundred tigers this way.

Once we drove far into the mountains on the Maharajah's private roads to Chail and Kufri. The Maharajah guarded his mountain estates jealously, and these roads were without exception closed to public traffic. It was said that only Gandhi and the Viceroy of India had travelled here before us, apart from the Maharajah and his employees, of course. This time we did not use the motorcycle but Father Johannssen's official car, and I was glad to be only a passenger because of the many bends in the road. The driver, a merry and cheerful Indian, drove like a madman, although he knew the road like the back of his hand. We begged Father Johannssen to tell him to slow down, as we were terrified and feeling sick.

"If he slows down," said Johannssen, "then he'll lose his nerve. I've been trying for a year to hold him back a bit, but it's no good, and no other driver will risk himself on this road."

Even Father Johannssen was rather green about the gills when we reached our destination, but after all, there are drawbacks in any job, and Father Johannssen only had to go to Chail once a month.

Here we could see the mighty peaks of the Himalaya right in front of us. Here Tibetan elements were already visible in the land, and we found a Tibetan temple with prayer flags fluttering in the wind. Only a hundred kilometres lay between us and the border with Tibet, and with it the Chinese empire. We stayed a long time on the mountain top, looking north. Out there lay a new world for us, more forbidding, more exotic, and consequently more attractive than any we had known so far. Both of us were very quiet on the way back, and I suspect that this afternoon was the origin of our subsequent travels which were to take both of us to China.

Our contemplative silence suffered one dramatic interruption. Fortified by a long rest and probably eager to get back to his young wife, our driver was going at a pace which made our journey out seem a mere stroll by comparison. Most of the corners we rounded not just on the proverbial two wheels but with *three* hanging out over the precipice. Suddenly we were overtaken by a strange round-shaped animal that went bounding away down the road in front of us. The driver was well-trained; he stopped the car with a jolt that sent the blood to our heads and our hearts into our mouths. Father Johannssen raised his rifle and took aim. There were all kinds of predators hereabouts, such as wild dogs, which it was his job to shoot down. We all watched the animal as it scurried away. It continued along the road for a bit, then with a mighty bound it leapt at a rock and then sped back up the road in the opposite direction to the one it had been escaping in. After a couple of convulsions it lay down and stopped. It looked remarkably circular – it was in fact our left back wheel.

After the runaway had been retrieved and firmly screwed back on again, Father Johannssen took the steering wheel and we drove home at a comfortable snail's pace. The Indian wearing a martyred expression as if he were being burned at the stake.

Even the happy days at Vaikunth came to and end and we had to go on. We had registered at the university in Vienna, even though we were absent, and they were waiting for us as were the Puch Works, so we could not allow ourselves to lose all sense of time.

The four Johannssens stood waving goodbye, Vaikunth disappeared behind a hill, and we were back on the road.

*VISIT VELOCE ON THE WEB – WWW.VELOCE.CO.UK*
*All current books • New book news • Special offers • Gift vouchers • Forum*

*163*

# 20
# CROSSING INDIA

As we coasted quietly down the road with the engine off, the days at Vaikunth passed before my eyes again like a kaleidoscope. The glorious sunrises that we could watch without getting out of bed; the days of cool air and hot sun; the great deep nights with their special Asian atmosphere.

I remember one night in particular. The drumming had begun that afternoon: always the same rhythm, swelling, falling away, then a short pause and the same rise and fall repeated. This went on for hours. We followed the sound to a high mountain meadow where several hundred peasants were holding a kind of fair. There were wrestling matches (India's national sport), sideshows, everything you'd expect at a local fête. Several small babies had been 'parked' by their mothers under a spring, and the women had invented a cooling system that would probably fill mothers in other parts of the world with horror. A fine stream of water was directed through a bamboo tube on to the child's head, so that they could enjoy the benefits of the hot sunshine without getting sunstroke. We got back to Vaikunth late in the evening, but the drumming continued all through the night until just before dawn. The fairground jollity gave way to mystic ceremonial, and the outsider, seen kindly as a spectator in the daytime, was driven off as an unwelcome interloper. We had no idea what went on in the mountain meadow at night, what gods were worshipped or what sacrifices performed, but the drum rhythm that had sounded so cheerful in the afternoon grew menacing and fanatical.

It still echoed in my ears as we slipped down towards the plain, but I could not allow myself to dream. The road demanded my full attention. Never-ending processions of buffalo carts moved along it: hundreds upon hundreds of vehicles. They were heavily laden, but I could not make out what goods they were taking to the mountains. They were certainly on their way to Simla, the summer capital of the British-Indian government. It lay further up the mountain beyond Solon, and thanks to its existence we had another good road.

India has indeed two capitals, at least, it used to have, for the National Government of India has done away with this luxury. What appeared justifiably as a luxury to the Indians, was actually a necessity for the Europeans. In Delhi, the real capital and the site of the magnificent Viceregal Palace, it is so hot during the summer that Europeans find it difficult to work. So the British made the generous decision to

After the weary agony of Persia and Baluchistan, India provoked in us an outburst of high spirits. We thought it would be a really bright idea to teach an Indian fakir how to ride a motorcycle!

transfer the government to Simla in summer. Even an Indian July is bearable at an altitude of two thousand metres, and that is how little Simla became a political and social centre. Ladies in evening gowns and gentlemen in dinner jackets became part of the normal evening scene. Now Simla will go back to being what it once was – an idyllically beautiful little town with incomparable views of the hazy Indian plains and the snow giants of Tibet.

Soon we were once again enveloped in the hot air of the plains. Even now, just a few weeks before Christmas, it was oppressively hot. The change of temperature made us tired, and we soon began to look around for somewhere to spend the night. As the towns are very far apart and the smaller places can offer only miserable little inns, this was not always easy. Even if we had not been put off by the poverty of the inns, we would not have been welcome guests. Religion is everything in India. Some inns are only open to Moslems, others only to Sikhs, others again are only for Brahmans, or for members of other castes, and the untouchables, or pariahs, have to sleep somewhere outside the village. We would have caused consternation among the good people of any township if we had wanted to spend the night there. Even if they had found somewhere for us to sleep which would not have been defiled too greatly by our presence, who could have given us food? Which water would we have been permitted to drink? Even on railway stations, where a slight air of modernity has the effect of relaxing the strict laws of the villages, there are always two taps for drinking water, one labelled 'For Hindus Only' and the other 'For Mohammedans Only.'

In spite of the difficulties and the dangers we presented, people in general were very hospitable. One morning when we crawled out of our tent, we found two earthenware pots of curdled milk and bread outside. Several peasants were crouched at a suitable distance. They must have smashed the pots afterwards, since they would have become unusable from their contact with unclean persons like us. We really felt almost like lepers. When making a purchase from an especially pious shopkeeper – and they were only too keen to do business with us – we had to lay our coins on the counter, since he would never have taken them directly from our hands.

The question of overnight accommodation would therefore have been difficult to resolve without the 'Dak' bungalows. These rest houses, which are run by the government, can be found at regular intervals along the main roads, even in the most isolated areas. They were mainly for the use of government employees, but private travellers might also put up there. Whilst the hotels in the big cities charged very high prices, one paid only a small sum at the rest houses for a room and an English meal, which was excellently cooked.

Like many other Indian cities, Delhi also consists of two strictly separate parts. New Delhi has the Parliament, the Viceregal Palace, most of the public buildings and the European bungalows. It is a modern garden city, laid out in the style of Washington with enormous distances. In Old Delhi are found the residence of the Great Mughal, the Fort, and what is claimed to be the largest mosque in the world. We stayed in New Delhi which lies at a distance of about ten kilometres from Old Delhi. Some businesses were in Old Delhi and some in our part of the city, so that in spite of using our vehicle it could take half a day to get around between the post office, the hotel and the photographer's. We caused a sensation with our motorcycle in both Old and New Delhi. Although bicycles were widespread, motorcycles were still a rarity. We were soon besieged by reporters and photographers wanting details of our journey and what we were going to do next.

We were overwhelmed by the huge number of newspapers in India. This probably has in part something to do with the Indian mentality: Indians love discussing and philosophising, and the newspaper is an expression of that delight in mental activity.

Unfortunately our plan to meet Gandhi did not come off. He was away on a political propaganda trip at the time, on a route far from any of the roads we would be on, preaching the All-India unification of all castes and religions.

Soon after Delhi, the fine tarmac road which we had followed all the way across India came to an end and gave way to a wretched fourth class country road, crumbling from over-use. It's just a myth that there are only good roads in India. On the contrary, most are in very poor condition, and it is only in zones of military importance that the lines of communication are maintained to a high standard. Thus there was a first-class tarmac road leading over the Khyber Pass (the famous, nay notorious, frontier pass between India and Afghanistan), with another road of equal excellence running parallel to it. Since the south had no military significance, its roads were neglected.

We would have been glad to make more rapid progress, as the landscape was somewhat lacking in attraction – a sun-scorched plain with a few sparse paddy fields and small stock of trees, although countless little rivers and brooks ran through it, creating stands of lush vegetation along their banks. The road traffic was surprisingly heavy, but it was not the kind of traffic we had expected on the main route to Bombay. We scarcely ever met a motor vehicle, although there were hundreds of buffalo carts and even a few little carts drawn by camels. Buffaloes, camels and their drivers all regarded the roadway as their ancient inherited domain, and nothing would induce them to give way by as much as a foot, although we sounded the horn and shook our fists threateningly. I am convinced that there was no malice in their behaviour, it was just that they could not imagine that we might be in a greater hurry than they were.

Pedestrians were the worst of all. Some peasants were sufficiently impressed to stand aside for us, amazed and open-mouthed. They were slow and hesitant but at least they moved over. The pilgrims and fakirs, some of whom were nearly naked and smeared with ashes, simply didn't notice us at all. They were so deep in thought and their minds so far away that their legs just moved automatically along the dusty road. Was it reasonable to expect legs alone to recognise our priority?

Sometimes a cloud of dust would enliven the leisurely moving traffic which even we did not disturb very much. Usually this was not a motor car but a racing dromedary ridden by two people, picking its way with surprising skill between the human obstacles.

All this would have been bearable, had it not been for the cows. These sacred animals, sometimes painted all over their bodies with mysterious writing and symbols, trotted along in a line or as a herd. Perfectly well aware that they were sacred and could not be injured, they stared at us contemptuously as we tried to worm our way through their ranks. No Hindu would have dared to drive them out of the way, either with a stick or just a little shove. If they had been cosseted in this way for hundreds or maybe thousands of years, how could we expect our nervous hooting to have any effect on them? They probably thought it was just a new form of worship!

There was a practical reason for this overcrowding on the roads and the absence of motor traffic. Indian railways are so cheap and the network is so extensive that it is scarcely worth travelling by motor vehicle, which in many places is regarded as a luxury.

In Agra we saw the Taj Mahal, of course. It was hard to approach without a degree of scepticism. We had seen it in films – mostly rather kitschy ones. Coloured postcards (the curse of all tourism) had promised us lily-white marble. Its various epithets 'Monument to a great love,' 'A dream in marble', and 'The most beautiful building in the world' had given us a strong aversion to cheap superlatives.

"But," we told ourselves, "if we are in Agra, we have to see it. We have no choice."

So one hot and sunny afternoon, we rode out to the site of the mausoleum, which is a veritable town. We were dusty, tired and hungry and we were longing for a cool Dak bungalow.

Then we saw the Taj Mahal.

Until now I have not found it particularly difficult to describe our trip and our impressions. I even think that my portrayal of the magnificent deserts and bare mountains and the effect they had on us should allow any reader with enough imagination to share our feelings. But now ...

How can I begin to describe this building with a few pathetic words? Its uniqueness, its beauty, I might almost say its holiness, are such that it can be seen, felt, worshipped – but not described, except by a poet. I am certainly no poet, and since I have no wish to take refuge in the usual superlatives, I would rather tell the story of what we did, quite objectively.

We had already filled our tank ready for the next part of the journey and we arrived in the afternoon, intending just to 'drop by.' In fact, we spent the entire afternoon sitting in the cool shade of the park surrounding the Taj, and couldn't stop looking. We said very little because we couldn't find the right words. In the evening twilight the scene grew even more unreal. We wandered through the park, still looking at the Taj.

Then night fell. The moon was nearly full. They say that the Acropolis is at its most beautiful by moonlight, and probably every marble building is enhanced by the soft light of our nocturnal satellite. To begin with we had found it impossible to imagine anything finer than the Taj, radiant and gleaming in the sunlight. Then we saw it as an ivory silhouette against the purple of evening, but when we at last came face to face with the Taj by moonlight, we knew that we had judged too soon.

We were not the only nocturnal visitors to the park. Many Indians were there, sitting about alone or in silent groups, enjoying it as we did. I have seldom felt such affection for Indians as at that moment. They are normally a garrulous people who love to talk, but confronted with this sight, they grew silent and reverent, as we do in church. How terrible if there had been chattering groups and courting couples secretly whispering! But I warmed to these silent Indians.

We were on our way before daybreak. We knew now that nothing could surpass the sight of the Taj Mahal by moonlight, and we did not want the new day to ruin the picture for us.

We had intended to get at least as far as Gwalior that day, but conditions along the way defeated our intentions. Creepers, ferns, tall grasses, thick bushes and treacherous swamps where the road would suddenly disappear hindered our progress. After a long day spent manoeuvring the heavily loaded machine this way and that, night overtook us during an extended cigarette break. We tried to keep going through the jungle by the light of our headlamp. Round about there were ghostly shadows and crackings and rustlings in the bushes. We could see nothing, not even the traditional glowing eyes of predators, but all the same we felt uneasy. Then the machine skidded, and we found ourselves immobilised with a puncture into the bargain. There was no question of doing a repair in the darkness, so we had no choice but to put up our tent. We did so without speaking a word. No doubt Herbert was just as afraid as I was, but since he said nothing, neither did I. The jungle in Gwalior is full of game and a highly-regarded hunting ground for tiger and panther. We knew perfectly well that we had little to fear from these big cats, since only in very rare cases do they attack human beings. Usually they give us a very wide berth – but not always. There are the so-called 'man-eaters' which acquire the taste for human flesh by chance and thereafter prefer it to any other meat. Where one of these man-eaters threatens the jungle area along a main road, the fact is usually advertised with warning notices. We had seen no such notices, but for all we knew, man-eaters might sometimes make excursions into unmarked territory.

We stretched the mosquito net across the entrance to our tent with extreme care.

A typical encounter on Indian roads: a sadhu (penitent and pilgrim) on his way to a shrine in the Himalaya.

It was meant to protect us from snakes and other creepy-crawlies. We got out the little packet of gunpowder with which to burn out snake-bites, presented to us by Father Johannssen. We had accepted this somewhat radical remedy with amusement at the time. Now we remembered the deep burn scars we had seen on the legs of more than one Indian who had been lucky enough to be carrying one of these little packets in an emergency.

In spite of being so tired, we were unable to get to sleep for a long time. Our ears pricked up at every rustling in the lianas and at the hoarse screeching of the monkeys in the treetops. Seldom have we longed so desperately for the first rays of the sun, or rejoiced so greatly when they arrived as we did after this night in the jungle.

*VISIT VELOCE ON THE WEB – WWW.VELOCE.CO.UK*
*All current books • New book news • Special offers • Gift vouchers • Forum*

*170*

We were overwhelmed by the sight of the Taj Mahal in Agra, the famous 'monument to a great love,' and could not tell whether it was more beautiful in bright sun or by moonlight. 20,000 craftsmen worked for nearly 20 years on this magnificent mausoleum of white marble with its lotus dome, erected by Shah Jahan in 1648.

# 21
# THE WISH LIST

Our route onwards to Bombay now took us through several princely states – Gwalior, Bhopal, and Indore. The private secretary of the Maharanee of Gwalior had written to us at Solon (an Indian friend had recommended us to him) informing us that Her Highness the Maharanee had commanded him to offer us every assistance when visiting her domains, and that he awaited instructions as to our arrival and what we wished to see. This letter sounded formal rather than sincere, and in fact we were received with such very impersonal hospitality in Gwalior that we rode on again after two days. Yet again we were overwhelmed by the indescribable pomp, the extravagant displays of luxury and the accumulation of treasures which are the hallmark of these little feudal states. We felt even then that the contrast between wealth and poverty in India was too glaring, too unbearable to last long in these modern times of awakening consciousness.

Indore turned out to be a most delightful and engaging episode in our trip. The young Maharajah, who had a special liking for American and European ladies, was away at the time on his travels in the countries of the West, but his private secretary had written to us in the warmest terms, inviting us to take full advantage of the guest palace and of his services, whenever it should please us and for as long as we wished.

Arriving in the city, we asked the first Sikh we met for directions to the palace. He looked at us and at the motorcycle for a moment and said, "Oh, you're from Austria! Now which one of you is from Vienna and which one from the Tyrol? I've been reading all about you in the papers!" This struck us as a good omen and we made our way to the palace in good spirits. We were met there by a charming old gentleman. He introduced himself as the Maharajah's private secretary, "A high caste Hindu, like the Maharajah himself. But for you, my young friends from Europe, I am neither a Hindu nor secretary to His Highness. Consider me as your advisor, friend and philosopher!"

The Philosopher, as we called him from then on, showed the most touching concern for us. He took us to a palace where each of us had a suite of five rooms and a string of six servants at our disposal. On each of our writing desks lay a little tear-off pad of forms printed clearly as follows:

The elephant god Ganesh, one of the thousand Hindu gods. The gigantic statue is richly decorated with gold and jewels.

There is more to India than the jungle. Here in northern India are open plains and lakes with idyllic little Hindu temples.

I desire on the … … … … … … …. at … … … … … …. o'clock:

1 Saddle Horse
1 Shooting Brake
1 Car
1 Elephant

… … … … … … … … … … … … … … … … … … … … … … … … … … ….

… … … … … … … … … … … … … … … … … … … … … … … … … … ….

(Please cross out which does not apply)

We crossed out what did not apply and were back in a dreamlike existence. We dined at richly laden tables, we slept in four-poster beds. Is it any wonder that after a few days we were assailed by thoughts and desires that would not have entered our wildest dreams on our exhausting journey through Persia and Baluchistan? Then it occurred to us that there were a couple of empty lines on the printed forms and we wondered what these might possibly bring us in India, land of miracles.

There was only one problem – the rest of our luggage, the problem being that it did not exist. In the pathetically small cases either side of the back wheel, we each had a spare shirt, spare pair of shorts, and as the centrepiece of our wardrobe, the famous plus-fours that had already caused such a stir in Teheran. It was a modest set of attire which filled only a tiny corner of the three clothes chests available to us at the palace.

Immediately after our arrival, the kindly Philosopher asked, "And the rest of your luggage? Is it coming by train?"

We were still so thoroughly awed by the five rooms and the pad of order forms that we both answered simultaneously, "Yes." It was a faint and not very convincing yes, but it was a yes all the same and we couldn't get out of it.

"Might I have the receipt so that the servant can go to the station?" requested the Philosopher.

Having said A, we were committed to B, and so we searched our wallets, leafed through our travel documents and put on a complete show. Feigning great consternation, we admitted we had lost the luggage ticket. What a piece of bad luck, what should we do now?

"Have no fear," said the Philosopher consolingly, "Have no fear at all. We'll soon run your luggage to earth. Where did you register it?"

"In Delhi," we affirmed.

Telephone calls were made to Delhi, to Bombay, and to various stations in between. We grew very nervous. Every other day we would go to the station at Indore and express anger at the negligence of Indian railways. The Philosopher comforted us as best he could, and when we departed a week later, we left precise instructions behind as to where he should forward our luggage. It was a sad, pathetic comedy which we played, and for all I know, the Philosopher was playing the comedy on his own account out of politeness.

Guests of the Maharajah of Indore. We get off the motorcycle and mount an elephant which carries a ladder for the purpose.

The tame cheetahs of the Maharajah of Gwalior are taken for their daily walk along the road by their keepers.

The Maharajah of Indore received us like royalty. Each of us had a five-roomed apartment. One is liable to dream and wish for things that would have been unimaginable under stress out in the desert. Six of the palace servants were assigned solely to us! It was not so easy to keep these people occupied, as well as behaving as if we were thoroughly used to having servants around us all the time back home. The photo shows me in conversation with our Indian 'friend, advisor and philosopher' at the maharajah's court. I would summon our servants every morning early and we would discuss how to employ them.

The man seemed to be an eloquent and convincing orator and he would hold forth to us for hours on every conceivable Indian problem. If we had given unconditional credence to everything he said, and if events had not on several occasions proved his theories drastically wrong, we would have come back to Europe with some totally false ideas about a single united India.

I have a particularly clear recollection of one very pleasant evening with whisky and cigarettes, when the Philosopher attempted to prove to us that the caste spirit no longer existed in India.

"Look at me," he said, "I am a high caste Hindu. According to the outdated rules of my caste, I should not be permitted to take meals with you, but I do so gladly and it does not bother me at all. You are Christians and Europeans, I am a Hindu and an Indian – but are we not more than just human beings and brothers, are we not friends?"

It nearly brought tears to our eyes, and this encouraged the Philosopher to make a fatal assertion.

"Yes," he declaimed, with tears in his own eyes, "even the pariahs, who are considered unclean by old-fashioned Hindus, even they are my brothers. There are no castes, there are only Indians! Remember this when you return to Europe."

Herbert got up and went out. A moment later he returned, dragging behind him into the room a reluctant 'sweeper.' Sweepers are pariahs whose task is to clean the washrooms and latrines, which in India are still primitive, with no water. These people are considered very unclean and are the lowest of the low in the towering structure of castes. The Philosopher had his back turned towards Herbert and did not hear him come in, since his declarations of brotherly love were just reaching a peak of volubility.

Herbert laid a hand on his shoulder and shoved the sweeper into the circle of light cast by the low-standing lamp.

"Here is one of your brothers," he said, "so shake him by the hand."

The full flow of the Philosopher's oratory was cut short by a strangled cry. We saw a fleeing shadow, then another one – and found ourselves alone. Both the Philosopher and the sweeper had hurtled from the room, deeply appalled by Herbert's experiment. The Philosopher remained out of sight for a whole day, delegating his duties to a less loquacious secretary. When he reappeared, he was all smiles and assailed us with a torrent of explanations. We must excuse his unconventional and abrupt departure. He had been overcome by a sudden nausea. He had spent the previous day at the doctor's, but was now in perfect health. Perhaps we would like to hunt some gazelle?

The other secretary, who had not said much, informed us later that the Philosopher had spent a very long day being washed clean by Brahman priests from the pollution caused by the proximity of the sweeper.

Had it not been for the business with the 'rest of our luggage' and the everlasting gazelle hunts, we would have counted our days in Indore among our happiest and most carefree. I have already mentioned the gazelle hunts. In spite of the efforts of the beaters and the tameness of the animals, which was an insult, we absolutely failed to shoot a single one. It was most humiliating.

One day we crossed out what did not apply for the last time on our 'wishlist' and bade a sad farewell to Indore.

The Philosopher accompanied us by car as far as the state frontier, and there were moist eyes all round as we shook hands with him. He may have been an unreliable philosopher and a poor advisor, but he was a good friend to us.

Only a few hundred kilometres more, and we were in Bombay. By now our thoughts dwelt constantly on home. We imagined a really grand and romantic homecoming, and as it turned out later, this was not so far from the truth.

When we reached the *Spinnerin am Kreuz* in Vienna on a cold day in January, there really was a crowd of people to meet us. There were kisses, photographs, laurel wreaths, embraces, interviews, and a shot for the newsreels. One or two managing directors even came too. For a short while we felt really important and just like heroes.

Indian architecture is not characterised only by the great palaces of the maharajahs, the magnificent Hindu temples or Mughal mosques. There are also innumerable smaller buildings of great charm, as here in Bombay, our final destination.

*Below:* On the return journey by ship from Bombay to Trieste we stopped off at Massaua in Eritrea at the famous salt-pans on the Red Sea.

*Above:* After India's heat, Europe's winter. We are wretchedly cold and have padded ourselves out with newspaper. Herbert has made himself some warm footwear. The India Expedition gives a thoroughly pathetic impression at the Italian-Austrian border at Tarvis.

Entering Vienna. A lot of people had turned out, including the board of the ÖTC (Austrian Touring Club) and even a minister. With the fully-laden machine, steering with one hand, I demonstrate riding on tramlines, as I learned in Istanbul.

Herbert Tichy and Max Reisch on the 'India Puch,' our indefatigable motorcycle. We are being greeted by His Excellency Meyr-Tenneberg (in fur cap), president of the ÖTC (today the ÖAMTC). Even amid the turmoil of these scenes of welcome, the stern engineers from the Puch Works were already examining the lead seals, all of which were in place and undamaged. I was truly proud of this, and we all shook hands with great satisfaction.

The 'India Puch' 250, 6 HP 1933 – The first motorcycle to reach India by the land route; a decisive impetus to the opening of Asia to road traffic.

*Right:* Over the next 50 years the expedition machine, the 'first motorcycle on the land route to India' was often loaned to museums, to motor club exhibitions, and was also exhibited in sports shops and bookshops. The 'India Puch' is still completely intact.

Max Reisch, one of the first collectors of veteran vehicles, kept all the motorcycles and cars from his travels. They are kept in running order by the Reisch-Orient-Archiv and from time to time appear in exhibitions. They are shown above and on the following pages.

Puch 175, 3HP 1931 – The first long-distance trip and written description of travel in Europe.

Sahara Puch T3, 6HP 1932. Desert trip through Morocco, Algeria, Tunisia and Libya.

Steyr 100. Used on the 1935-36 Trans-Asia Expedition and round-the-world trip. Max Reisch on the right with his wife, Christiane and son, Peter (1981).

Gutbrod 'Sadigi.' 1952. The first crossing of Saudi Arabia with a specially insulated camper van, the first in Europe.

Opel 'Moses.' 1958. The Austria Alexander Expedition. In the footsteps of Alexander the Great with Opel caravan and Touricamp car tent.

Ford 17M. 1961. In the footsteps of the Crusaders, the greatest towed-caravan expedition to the Orient.

With all these pleasant feelings, I went into college the next day. Of course, officially I had never been away, and I hoped the professors would turn a blind eye, considering that I had been reaping fame and recognition for Austria.

The first lecture where I put in an appearance was economic geography. "We shall have some tests today," said the professor with a benevolent glance at me. "We especially look forward to testing those gentlemen who have been to see a bit of the world for themselves. Learning by observation in the field, that's what young people need."

My chest swelled and I beamed at him. I had so many interesting details to tell him about the exchange of goods between Persia and India, and the jewel in the crown of my knowledge was the massive opium smuggling operation over the Himalaya from India to China. I could draw a plan of the routes and give an exact account of the prices.

"Mr Max Reisch, if I remember rightly?" said the professor, giving me an even more benevolent look.

"Yes, sir!" I said, standing up.

"Are you ready to give us a short presentation?"

"Indeed, sir, yes, sir!"

"The subject of your presentation will be 'The principal exports of the State of Bolivia to Paraguay and their subsequent exploitation.' You have thirty minutes to speak on this subject."

I have never spoken so little in the course of half an hour. I said absolutely nothing. I had to repeat this course and many others in the following semester.

But the triumphs and disasters of homecoming were still in the lap of the gods as we covered our last few kilometres on Indian soil. The road was bad, wretchedly bad, but the skies above us were deepest blue, the air was fragrant and the palm-trees were fluttering in the breeze. I was inexpressibly happy. How wonderful the last months had been! What a glorious moment it was to have our destination in sight!

Round a bend in the road, a broad silvery streak appeared between the slim trunks of the palms, and ahead of us under a layer of smoke lay a big city – the sea and Bombay (now Mumbai).

"We're there," said Herbert.

"Thank Heaven," I said, and then, "More's the pity!"

And I truly did not know whether to be happy or sad.

We travelled home by ship from Bombay, via Aden and the Suez Canal to Trieste, and from there on our faithful motorcycle over the wintry roads to Vienna.

# 21
# WHAT HAPPENED NEXT?

So what happened to the 'India Puch' after it became famous for conquering the land route to India, the first motorised journey on Sven Hedin's caravan trail? The motorcycle I had grown to love was completely overhauled and did further good service on my subsequent journeys in Austria and Germany, and a longer trip to Great Britain and Scotland in the summer of 1934.

During the Second World War the companion of my many adventures lay safe in the cellars of the Vienna Technical Museum, after which I fetched it back to Kufstein to the garage of my home.

Here, the India Puch is the star of the Reisch-Orient-Archiv, managed by me with my son, Peter Reisch. We consider it our special task to give the youth of today an understanding of the excitement of travel, through lectures and exhibitions where the faithful India Puch, as ever, starts with a will and shows her paces.

**Max Reisch 1983**

## Postscript

My father died in 1985, since when I have continued to manage his legacy in the same spirit, together with *my* son, Peter A Reisch. The India Puch remains at the heart of the Reisch-Orient-Archiv, now in Bozen (Bolzano) in the South Tyrol in Italy. We service it regularly, and it is often in demand for filming and exhibitions.

The numerous other vehicles from Max Reisch's journeys have been preserved, and are kept safe in this collection, unique in the world, comprising the expedition vehicles of a transport pioneer.

As well as the motorcycles and automobiles with their original equipment, the Max Reisch Collection includes a large number of historic photographs and original films from his long-distance travel in the deserts of Africa and Asia.

We often show the exhibits to people who are interested, although a suitable location for a museum has yet to be found.

**Peter H Reisch 2010**
**Reisch-Orient-Archiv**

*Also from Veloce Publishing Ltd –*

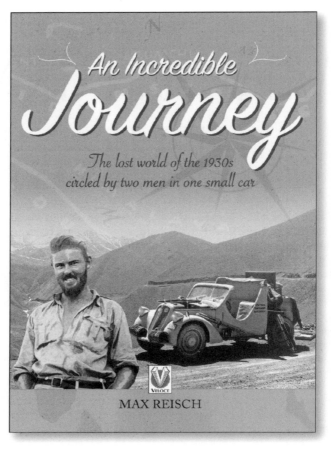

The compelling story of Max Reisch and Helmuth Hahmann's journey across Asia in 1935 in a Steyr 100. It is a story of adventure and discovery, revealing the countries, people and problems that they encountered along the way. With stunning period photographs, this book provides a historic and fascinating insight into a pre-WW2 world.

ISBN: 978-1-787111-65-3
Paperback • 21x14.8cm • 288 pages • 231 pictures

For more information and price details, visit our website at www.veloce.co.uk • email: info@veloce.co.uk • Tel: +44(0)1305 260068

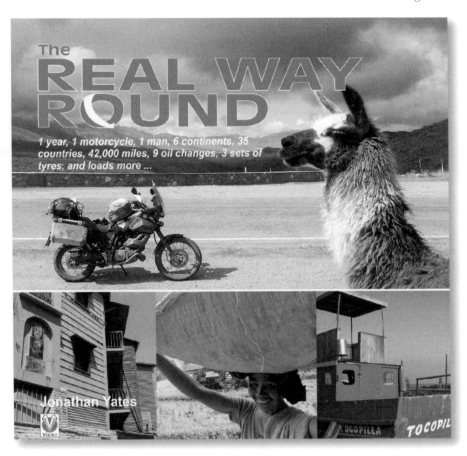

A pictorial diary of a once-in-a-lifetime motorcycle trip across 35 countries on a Yamaha Ténéré XT660, and a practical guide to motorcycling round the world – what to do first, what to plan for, and how to cope with the unexpected. Features stunning photography, details of bike modifications, route maps, points of interest, and practical guidance on freighting a bike.

ISBN: 978-1-845842-94-9
Hardback • 25x25cm • 224 pages • 692 colour pictures

For more information and price details, visit our website at www.veloce.co.uk • email: info@ veloce.co.uk • Tel: +44(0)1305 260068

*Also from Veloce Publishing Ltd –*

This is the story of an independent trek in a 50-year-old Mini – all the way to the Great Pyramid and back – with no assistance or support crew, to provide much needed funds and publicity for the Willow Foundation.

Inspirational to others, the book includes practical advice on the car preparation and documentation required for such marathon drives, along with photographs of the Mini's preparation and the amazing journey itself.

ISBN: 978-1-845843-61-8
Hardback • 25x20.7cm • 128 pages • 95 colour pictures

For more information and price details, visit our website at www.veloce.co.uk • email: info@ veloce.co.uk • Tel: +44(0)1305 260068

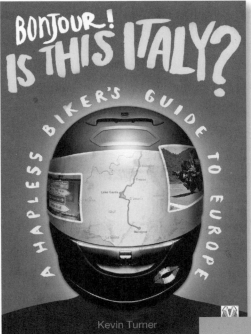

Following his dismissal from a job he never should have had, the author packs a tent, some snacks, and a suit, and sets out on a two-wheeled adventure across Europe. With no idea where he's going, and only two very large and confusing maps to rely on, he heads out to prove that planning and forethought are the very antithesis of a motorcycle adventure.

ISBN: 978-1-845843-99-1

Paperback • 21x14.8cm • 144 pages • 129 colour and b&w pictures

Critically acclaimed author Kevin Turner (*Bonjour! Is This Italy? A Hapless Biker's Guide to Europe*) heads off on another ill-thought out adventure, this time aiming his heavily laden Kawasaki north towards the towering waterfalls of Norway, before heading east on a long and treacherous journey to Moscow. This fascinating adventure – part sprint, part marathon – charts the perils, pitfalls and thrills of a 6000 mile solo motorcycle journey across Europe, Scandinavia and into Asia. The author's observations and anecdotes transform this motorcycle guidebook into a laugh-a-minute page turner, which inspires and entertains in equal measure.

ISBN: 978-1-845846-22-0

Paperback • 21x14.8cm • 160 pages • 134 colour pictures

# INDEX

VISIT VELOCE ON THE WEB – WWW.VELOCE.CO.UK
All current books • New book news • Special offers • Gift vouchers • Forum